THE
SKY'S
THE
LIMIT

JOHN P. CALAMOS, SR.

FOUNDER, CALAMOS INVESTMENTS

THE
SKY'S
THE
LIMIT

LESSONS IN SERVICE, ENTREPRENEURSHIP, AND ACHIEVING THE AMERICAN DREAM

JOE GARNER

NEW YORK TIMES BESTSELLING AUTHOR

WILEY

Published by John Wiley & Sons, Inc., Hoboken, New Jersey.
Published simultaneously in Canada.

For general information on our other products and services or for technical support, please contact our Customer Care Department within the United States at (800) 762-2974, outside the United States at (317) 572-3993 or fax (317) 572-4002.

Wiley also publishes its books in a variety of electronic formats. Some content that appears in print may not be available in electronic formats. For more information about Wiley products, visit our web site at www.wiley.com.

Library of Congress Cataloging-in-Publication Data:

ISBN: 9781394304028 (Hardback)
ISBN: 9781394304035 (ePub)
ISBN: 9781394304042 (ePDF)

Cover Design: Wiley
Cover Images: © Wesley Mann/AUGUST,
                © Gabriele Maltinti/Adobe Stock
SKY10099107_030325

Contents

Preface

The life of John Calamos is the embodiment of the American Dream—a journey that demonstrates how hard work, intuition, and a sense of duty can lead to extraordinary success.

This book chronicles not just the milestones of his life and career but also the values and principles that guided him along the way. Success, as John himself might say, leaves clues, and what you'll find in these pages is a collection of those clues, offering a map that could guide your own path.

John is the son of a Greek immigrant father and first-generation Greek American mother, both of whom instilled in him a deep pride in his heritage. Together, they taught him a strong work ethic, a profound appreciation for opportunity, and the understanding that prioritizing customer care leads to success.

His path to prosperity began with a chance discovery of old stock certificates—an event that awakened a passion for finance and set him on a course that would define his life's work.

But John's journey wasn't just about building a business; it was about serving his country, too. Inspired by President John F. Kennedy's famous words, "Ask not what your country can do for you, but what you can do for your country," he served in the US Air Force, even as the Vietnam War was escalating. There, he discovered another passion—flying—one that would stay with him for life.

John's courage and dedication shone brightly during his time as a forward air controller in Vietnam, a role that demanded not only skill but also immense bravery. For his service, he was awarded the Distinguished Flying Cross, a testament to his heroism. It was a dangerous job, but John embraced it with the same steadfast commitment that he would later bring to his career in finance.

His experiences in the cockpits of military aircraft ranging from the tiny Cessna O-2 Skymaster all the way up to the massive B-52 bomber taught him a way of thinking that played a crucial role in his success behind a very different set of controls—as the founder of Calamos Investments.

The calm and methodical decision-making and rational approach to emergencies he gained as a pilot helped his firm to come through turbulence like the Black Monday Crash of 1987 and the 2008 great financial crisis in one piece.

As a businessman, John's intuition often led him to buck conventional wisdom, but his unwavering focus on serving his clients always guided his decisions. For John, true success was measured not by his own achievements, but by the success of those he served.

His career is marked by a deep commitment to service—whether in the skies over Vietnam, the complex world of finance, or in giving back to the community through philanthropy and nonprofit leadership.

John is famously a quiet, humble man, never one to boast about his many accomplishments. Convincing him to share his story wasn't easy, but with his trademark modesty, he opened up, allowing me a glimpse into his extraordinary life.

To truly capture the full measure of John's story, I relied not only on him but also on the voices of those who know him best—his colleagues; Air Force reservist buddies; coworkers; his wife, Mae; his daughter, Laura; and other family members. Their insights revealed the depth of his character and provided a broader picture of the man behind the success.

By all measures, John Calamos has achieved the American Dream. And he has done so with a generosity of spirit, sharing his success with the people, institutions, and heritage that contributed to his remarkable journey.

His story is a powerful reminder that the road to success is paved not just with ambition but also with courage, integrity, and a willingness to give back.

I hope you find John's story as inspiring as I have.

—Joe Garner

Preface

Chapter 1

The American Dream: A Journey Begins

"You don't know where you're going unless you know where you came from."

—John P. Calamos, Sr.

A t the heart of America lies a fundamental truth: its population is made up of individuals from diverse corners of the globe. From the earliest settlers, including the nomads who crossed the Bering land bridge to become the first Native Americans, to those seeking refuge from persecution and countless others pursuing the promise of a brighter future, the American narrative is one of migration and hope. The journey of the Calamos family embodies this quintessential American tale.

In the early 1900s, as Europe stood on the brink of World War I, Greece faced the aftermath of the Balkan Wars amid a fragile geopolitical landscape. Internal divisions between monarchy and republicanism left the country's primarily agrarian economy offering little opportunity for its youth.

America was seen as a land of boundless opportunity, often referred to as the *golden land*. Stories of success and the chance to earn a living far beyond what was possible in Greece fueled dreams of a better life.

With America's industrial economy booming and a high demand for labor, immigrants found prospects for work and the ability to earn and save money—something nearly impossible in the struggling Greek economy.

The tale of the Calamos (Kalamoutsos) family finds its origin in the tranquil village of Vourvoura, nestled near the historic city of Tripoli on the Peloponnese peninsula in southern Greece.

Amid the timeless olive groves and vineyards unfolds the saga of a family whose journey would epitomize the essence of the American Dream.

In 1908, Evangelos Calamos, the patriarch of the family, answered America's call for promise. He was among nearly 40,000 Greek laborers recruited to work on railroads, mines, and mills across the country. Making multiple trips back and forth, he shared stories of America that ignited the ambitions of his son, Peter.

By 1914, young Peter Calamos, barely 17 years old, decided to follow in his father's footsteps and journey to America with a few friends from the village.

Beyond the economic challenges of their home country, the rising tumult that would soon lead to World War I made the challenges of immigration seem a worthy gamble.

With his parents' encouragement and support, Peter embarked on his journey, his dreams and apprehensions packed tightly alongside his sparse belongings. The ship sailed out into the vast Atlantic, but because his voyage coincided with the start of World War I, the ship had to cautiously hug the coastline to evade German U-boats until they were well out at sea.

It's easy to imagine that the nearly month-long voyage wasn't just about crossing from one continent to another. As the days passed, there would have been ample time for reflection, turning it into a journey of personal growth.

Finally catching sight of Lady Liberty must have been exhilarating, yet Ellis Island, still a mere mile off the US coastline, loomed as the last barrier before reaching America. Surrounded by the island's imposing structures and a constant stream of newcomers from every imaginable background, the scene was overwhelming.

Amid this mosaic of humanity, a cacophony of voices—young and old, speaking myriad languages—echoed throughout the large receiving hall, each voice carrying the weight of varied emotions: hope, fear, excitement, and apprehension.

Processing at Ellis Island was undoubtedly daunting, especially for someone as young as Peter. The entry conditions were strict, aimed at admitting only those who could contribute to the growing society of their new homeland. Dreams were scrutinized, and futures were decided in the course of just a few interviews.

On arrival, immigrants underwent a series of medical and legal inspections to ensure they did not pose a public health risk or become a burden on American society. The medical examination was the first critical hurdle, with doctors checking for diseases or disabilities that could prevent an individual from working.

This was followed by legal interviews, where officials verified documents and questioned immigrants about their backgrounds, financial status, and reasons for coming to America.

Immigrants had to prove they had a place to stay, some money, and that they would not likely become a public charge.

Once cleared, the weight of the new arrivals' journey gave way to exhilaration as they took their first steps on American soil—the land of boundless opportunity. With little more than the clothes on their backs, Peter and his friends from the village would have felt a rush of adventure as they set off for Ohio and the promise of manufacturing work the Midwest held.

The transition from the rustic, serene beauty of Greece to the industrial heartland of America was striking. Ohio's landscape, marked by its growing factories and the promise of employment, was a stark contrast to the life they had known.

They found work in one of these cathedrals of American industry, where the dreams of many immigrants were forged—and sometimes broken. However, the physical demands of their new roles were nothing compared to the social challenges they faced.

Greeks, Italians, Irish, and other immigrants were often met with suspicion and hostility, seen as outsiders in a nation grappling with its own identity. Slurs and prejudices were commonplace, serving as daily reminders that their acceptance was conditional, and their presence merely tolerated rather than embraced.

The factory became a crucible, testing the young men's resilience and shaping their understanding of the American work ethic.

It was amid the soot and clamor of production that tragedy struck—one of Peter's companions suffered a fatal accident. This pivotal moment in Peter's early life sparked a profound change, driving him to seek a new direction.

Leaving Ohio behind, Peter set his sights on Chicago. In this bustling metropolis, rich with a vibrant Greek community, he would plant the seeds of a legacy that would intertwine with the very fabric of America itself.

During this era, Chicago's population swelled, fueled by a steady influx of immigrants from Europe, including Greeks, Italians, and Eastern Europeans, along with a significant migration of African Americans from the South, part of the Great Migration.

These newcomers sought employment in the city's thriving factories, stockyards, and railroads, contributing to a vibrant yet sometimes strained cultural mix.

Economically, Chicago flourished as a center of manufacturing and meatpacking, with the Union Stockyards standing as a symbol of the city's industrial power. However, this prosperity came with its own set of challenges.

Socially and culturally, Chicago was lively, yet deeply divided by racial and ethnic lines.

Neighborhoods formed cultural enclaves where communities established networks of churches, schools, and social clubs.

Although segregation is often associated with racial divides, the ethnic distinctions in Chicago during that era were equally rigid. Peter quickly learned to navigate the boundaries separating Greek, Polish, and Italian neighborhoods.

Politically, this era was characterized by corruption and the growing influence of organized crime, which would come to the forefront during Prohibition in the 1920s. Notorious figures like Al Capone began their rise to power during this time, foreshadowing the city's ongoing struggle with the corruption, intimidation, and violence of organized crime in the decade ahead.

Chicago stood at a crossroads, embodying both the promise and contradictions of the American experience. Within this vibrant landscape, Peter found a sense of belonging in the city's expansive Greek community, which became a vital anchor for him. It offered not only a connection to his heritage but also essential support as he navigated his new life.

As Greek-owned businesses, cafés, and restaurants began to flourish, Greektown emerged as a lively hub. These establishments served as informal meeting places where community members could gather and share news from back home.

The melodic cadence of the Greek language mingled with the savory aromas of traditional cuisine—garlic, oregano, roasted lamb, and calamari—creating an atmosphere of comfort and evoking a profound sense of belonging.

Instead of seeking jobs in factories or stockyards, Peter chose the entrepreneurial path. His time in Ohio's factories had left a bad taste in his mouth, driving him toward self-employment. This decision would shape his family for generations, influencing the choices of his son, John.

Initially, he made a living by peddling produce, a practice that foreshadowed his eventual career in the grocery trade. Every morning, he would take a pushcart to the Fulton-Randolph District wholesale food market, buy fruits and vegetables, and then walk down the alley selling them to his neighbors.

Encouraged by the success of his fruit and vegetable cart, Peter saw an opportunity to better serve the needs of the growing community. He reached out to a few friends, and together they pooled their resources and expertise to start a small grocery store.

For Peter and his partners, this venture was more than just a business; it was a chance to build something meaningful that would set them firmly on the path to the American Dream.

The grocery store quickly became a neighborhood staple, offering not only essentials but also a gathering place where people could connect, share news, and find a taste of their homeland on the shelves. Peter and his partners worked tirelessly, their dedication evident in every aspect of the store—from the quality of the products to the warm, welcoming service they provided.

However, when the Great Depression hit in 1929 and lingered through the 1930s, their small business faced the harsh realities of widespread job loss, shrinking incomes, and economic instability.

Despite their best efforts to keep the store afloat, Peter and his friends had to confront the difficult truth: their business could not survive the economic storm. The closure of their grocery store marked a significant setback, ending a dream they had nurtured together.

Yet, this experience also highlighted their resilience, camaraderie, and the enduring hope that had brought them to America in the first place. It underscored the uncertainties of immigrant life and the vulnerabilities faced by small businesses during one of the most challenging periods in American history.

In the same Greek community in Chicago lived Mary Kyriako-poulos, the second eldest American-born daughter of Greek immigrants from near Tripoli. The tragedy of her parents' early deaths left her orphaned and burdened with the responsibility of caring for her six siblings.

Although only in her early twenties, Mary was already nearing what was considered the "old maid" age, a label that weighed heavily in the social context of the time. As fate would have it, a mutual friend saw an opportunity for both Peter and Mary. Knowing Peter was single, the friend recommended marriage—not to one of the younger Kyriakopoulos sisters, as Peter had initially thought, but to Mary herself.

Recognizing the potential for building a life together, Peter took the advice to heart, despite Mary being nearly 17 years his junior. They agreed to the plan and exchanged vows at The Assumption Panagia Greek Orthodox Church on Valentine's Day, 1937.

Within a year, Mary and Peter happily welcomed their first child, a son named Angelo. Just two years later, they celebrated the birth of another boy, John, followed by their daughter, Lorraine (Lori), in 1942. Between the births of John and Lori, Peter took a leap of faith and opened another grocery store.

In 1941, Pete and Mary Calamos proudly opened Pete's Food Market in a two-story brick building at 5145 West Division Street in westside Chicago's Austin neighborhood. Their store occupied the ground floor, while the family lived in the apartment above.

Despite the challenges of the era—economic strains from the war and simmering racial tensions—Austin in the early 1940s embodied the true essence of the American melting pot.

Ethnic groups, including Irish, Italian, German, Polish, and Greek families, coexisted, their cultures intertwining through community events, religious services, and neighborhood celebrations.

The American Dream: A Journey Begins

Amid this rich diversity, a spirit of resilience and community thrived, fueled by an unwavering belief in a brighter future. For a young John Calamos, growing up in this vibrant environment marked the beginning of his journey of growth and adaptation, shaping his outlook on life and influencing his aspirations for the future.

Chapter 2

Stock boy and the Stock Certificates

The Calamos family embodied the spirit of a typical working-class American family in early 1940s Chicago. Close-knit and industrious, Peter and Mary Calamos managed Pete's Food Market together, where Peter handled day-to-day operations and Mary divided her time between the store and managing their household.

She was a loving, no-nonsense mother to their three children and equally business-minded, often nudging Peter over his tendency to accept IOUs when neighbors made late-night grocery runs, exasperatingly reminding him, "We're trying to run a business; you can't give everything away!"

Their joint effort in running the store was the cornerstone of the family's life, shaping young John's understanding of customer service and business acumen. Mary's influence was particularly profound; it was she who would later provide John with the initial capital to start investing, reflecting her keen involvement in and understanding of the family's finances.

Although Peter and Mary were proud of their Greek roots, they were determined that their children would fully embrace American culture. Despite being fluent in Greek, they hardly ever spoke it at home, believing that immersing their children in English was key to their success.

Like many other Greek children in the area, John and his siblings, Angelo and Lori, attended Greek school at the nearby Greek Orthodox church on Saturdays to learn Greek and maintain a connection to their heritage.

Pete's Food Market was an indispensable part of the community, open seven days a week. Even during family dinners, they'd occasionally hear the doorbell ring as neighbors sought items they had neglected to pick up earlier in the day. Even though the store was closed for the day, Peter was always willing to run downstairs to get them what they needed, showing John at an early age just how vital it is to take good care of the customers.

Described as a "daredevil" by his older brother, Angelo, John was always getting into some mischief. As a young boy, while playing on the second story back porch, John suddenly imagined himself as Superman.

So, without thinking twice, he climbed up onto the balcony railing and took a leap, hoping to soar all the way to the nearby tree. But things didn't quite go as planned. Instead of reaching the tree limbs, he came crashing toward the ground.

Luckily, there was a clothesline stretched across the backyard, and it broke his fall. He managed to fling himself across it and hung there awkwardly until his brother came to his rescue and helped him down. With a mix of relief and amusement, the family often shared the story of John's daring stunts, a testament to his adventurous spirit and determination, starting at a young age.

When John reached school age, he attended John Hay Elementary School, the neighborhood public school located just two blocks from the Calamos home. Early on, John exhibited a strong sense of leadership and initiative.

He became a school safety guard, a role he embraced with great enthusiasm. His dedication earned him recognition and an award for exemplary conduct, leading to a pivotal experience that left a lasting impression on him. "When our principal took over as the head of all Chicago public schools, we, the patrol boys, got all dressed up and presented downtown," John recalled.

The ceremony, held in the superintendent's office, gave him a chance to experience an environment he'd never encountered before. The office, with its perfectly arranged desks and its dignified atmosphere, instantly captivated John. It stood in stark contrast to the familiar and casual settings of his everyday life. "I remember we were given a tour of the office, and I was so impressed by the superintendent's desk," John said.

The desk he saw was both physically impressive and symbolically significant. It was a large, stately piece, made of polished wood that gleamed under the office lights, commanding his attention. Everything about it was meticulously organized, reflecting professionalism and discipline. "That visit actually inspired me. When I was in high school, I took a woodworking class so I could build myself a desk. It all stemmed from that first experience seeing that office when I was younger," John recalled.

As soon as the final school bell rang each afternoon, John would quickly shift from student to a stock clerk, heading straight to the store. There, he and his siblings spent their afternoons stocking shelves and pitching in wherever their age and size allowed. "I grew up in the grocery store," John stated.

As John grew older, he started taking on more responsibilities at the store, including delivering groceries around the neighborhood. After the store closed for the day, he would head straight upstairs to tackle his homework and have dinner.

Before long, working at the family store became just one of John's many jobs. He eventually took on newspaper delivery routes and even washed the storefront windows of neighboring businesses. But the store was always the top priority.

Apart from the store, the Calamos family's life revolved around their close-knit extended relatives—including aunts, uncles, cousins, and close friends.

When it came to family gatherings, Mary handled most of the cooking and hosting duties. On Sundays, if the weather was good, the whole family would head to Long Lake for a day of fun and picnicking.

At that time, Long Lake, located about an hour outside of Chicago, was a picturesque retreat from urban life, surrounded by the natural beauty of rural Illinois. This serene setting, with its expansive tracts of farmland, dense woodlands, and the gently lapping waters of the lake, offered an ideal escape for both young and old in the family.

While the adults were busy preparing food and chatting about work, relatives, and friends, the children explored the nearby woods and splashed in the lake. The air was filled with the echoes of laughter and the mouthwatering smells of souvlaki or kebabs cooking on the grill.

From a young age, John's insatiable curiosity had him diving into the workings of every gadget and machine he encountered, eagerly unraveling them as if each were a fascinating puzzle waiting to be solved.

At 13, while cleaning the family's 1948 Ford, he discovered the car manual. Once he finished the wash, John became curious. He sat down and pored over the manual from cover to cover, fully absorbing the details about how to start the car, shift gears, and manage the brakes.

Feeling confident, he decided to test his newfound knowledge. He climbed behind the wheel, turned the key, and the Ford started right up, its engine humming. As he navigated his first time in the driver's seat, a sly, proud smile spread across his face.

Carefully, he put the car in reverse, maneuvering it out of the garage, shifted gears, drove it around to the street, and neatly parked it in front of the store. When his father stepped outside, he was surprised and wondered aloud, "How did the car end up here?"

A few years later, John purchased a used Pontiac as his very own car. Being secondhand, it naturally came with its share of problems. He ended up changing the carburetor three times, handling the repairs himself.

Working on the car became a hobby for John. He picked up new skills with each repair. He enjoyed his time in the garage with his head under the hood, learning and exploring, the sounds of tools clinking, and the gratification of each engine rev.

John had another reason for keeping his car in top condition: racing. He and his friends would tear through the streets of Chicago, their rivalry fueling a need to test the limits of their machines. John vividly described the scene: "You'd pull up to a light on North Avenue, size up the guy next to you," he reminisced.

Suddenly, engines roared, eager for the green light, and the moment it switched, John floored it, though he tempered his aggression, mindful that replacing parts was a cost he couldn't afford— classic risk management.

John's need for speed showcased his competitive streak, but the strong work ethic that permeated all other aspects of his life he attributed to his parents.

"My mother was the foundation of our household, always ensuring that we were well cared for and that our home was a welcoming and organized place," John recalls. "She managed everything from our daily meals to keeping the house tidy and making sure our needs were met, allowing us to focus on school and our other activities." John continued, "My dad would be up at four in the morning to buy produce at the Fulton-Randolph District wholesale food market for our store, and I was right there with him, helping out. I was always working."

Stock boy and the Stock Certificates

As John grew older, he felt a pull toward something bigger than what Chicago could offer. Then, one day, an unexpected discovery gave a sudden boost to his growing aspirations.

In a routine trip to the store basement to stow away an item, he stumbled on something that would change his path forever.

Amongst the clutter of forgotten items, he came across an old box nestled in a corner. Intrigued, he began rifling through its contents, and there, buried beneath layers of dust, he discovered old stock certificates dating from the 1920s and 1930s.

The intricate engravings around the borders and the stately looking company seals immediately drew John's attention. Initially, he was puzzled by his discovery. However, as he read over the certificates, seeing terms like *ownership*, the number of shares, and the date of purchase quickly turned his bewilderment into excitement.

Intrigued by the discovery of these formal-looking documents, John, hopeful he'd found a treasure, asked his father about the certificates. "Oh, they were left behind by a relative of ours who was passing through," Peter said.

John began researching the certificates, exploring the history of the companies that issued them and their fate during the Great Depression. Learning the certificates were worthless didn't dampen John's spirits; instead, it launched his interest in investing.

After thorough research, he chose five stocks that stood out for their strong fundamentals and growth potential: Texas Instruments, Thiokol Chemical Company, Brunswick, Beckman Instruments, and Muntz TV. These companies were among the top innovators of the time, a focus that has stayed with John throughout his investment career.

His mother, always supportive of his interests, was impressed by his impassioned and thorough approach, and allowed him to invest $5,000 from their family savings into these stocks. This marked a significant turning point in John's journey as an investor.

His stock picks generally fared well, although there was one notable exception. Muntz TV, the stock his cousin had recommended, did not perform as hoped. "It was a disappointment," John recalled. "You have to do your homework."

It became a valuable lesson John learned early on about the importance of trusting his research and instincts over "tips." Otherwise, it was a successful initial portfolio.

Before long, John's new hobby quickly turned into a true passion. His path to a career in finance started with an unexpected find in the basement of his family's store. Driven by his curiosity and a constant desire for learning, this discovery ignited his interest in investing.

However, it took some more time and several twists in his journey before he fully stepped into a career in the investment industry. But no doubt, this significant moment ultimately propelled him onto a path leading to places he never imagined.

Chapter 3

Factory Floors to Academic Halls

Throughout high school, John increasingly felt out of place in his Austin neighborhood. He knew he didn't want to end up running his father's grocery store. His growing interest in the stock market showed him a world of possibilities that seemed out of reach for most around him.

His chance visit to the school superintendent's office, filled with professionalism and ambition, also left a strong impression on him. Although he wasn't exactly sure where he was meant to go, he was certain his future was out there, somewhere far from where he started.

This belief was further reinforced during a pivotal summer job between his junior and senior years at Austin High School, where John spent long days working at the local Motorola factory.

He got the job through a connection; his friend's father managed the nearby facility on Augusta Boulevard. Financially, this job was an excellent opportunity for a teenager, offering a wage of $2 to $3 an hour, which was considered good money at the time.

John began his factory job fueled by typical teenage dreams, such as buying his first car. However, he quickly realized he was just a small cog in a loud, bustling assembly line, a sharp contrast to the customer interaction he enjoyed at his father's grocery store. Instead of assisting customers, he found himself plugging tubes into a seemingly endless stream of television sets, a monotonous task that offered little satisfaction.

He worked alongside factory workers hardened by years on the line who often scolded him for not keeping up. "They would shout at me to move faster, their voices cutting through the clatter of the machines," John recalled. "It made me feel a little conspicuous. I was constantly struggling to catch up." This relentless pace and the repetitive nature of the work only deepened his resolve to pursue a different path.

Initially, John put up with the summer job for the decent paycheck, but it quickly turned into a defining experience that shaped his future aspirations.

The tedious tasks and the sharp scent of machinery served as clear reminders of a life he was eager to escape. "Every day was the same, and each time, it just pushed me to think bigger, beyond those factory walls," John said with a chuckle.

Armed with a newfound sense of purpose, John entered his senior year with a life-changing question: Could college be his escape from a future of factory work? His goal to pursue higher education was more than just academic ambition; it was his way of declaring that he wanted a future shaped by his own aspirations, not by his circumstances.

Achieving this goal would not come without challenges. Like many immigrant families, higher education hadn't yet become part of the Calamos family's story.

Although his parents didn't have the opportunity to pursue higher education themselves, they wholeheartedly supported John's academic ambitions. In an era when family responsibilities often took precedence over education, their encouragement proved crucial.

With their support, along with guidance from his advisors, John applied to the University of Illinois (U of I) at the Navy Pier branch—known as the Chicago Undergraduate Division or humorously as "Harvard on the Rocks"—where he was subsequently accepted.

Established in 1946 to serve World War II veterans through the GI Bill, by 1959 it had evolved into a launchpad for Chicago-area students like John, including many first-generation college students.

However, John soon felt that the smaller branch campus wasn't giving him the robust collegiate experience he sought, and he requested a transfer to the main campus downstate in Champaign.

Once given the green light, John packed up and drove his car to the twin cities of Champaign-Urbana, marking the start of his real college experience at the largest college campus in the state. This move also represented the first time he had ever lived away from home, adding a layer of personal growth to his educational journey. He enrolled in the Reserve Officer Training Corps (ROTC), which was then a requirement for able-bodied males attending public universities in Illinois, selecting the Air Force service branch.

After two years at U of I, attending such a large university began to weigh on him. Sitting in massive lecture halls filled with hundreds of students made him feel lost in the crowd. "The main issue for me was the size," he explained. "Even back then, the school had about 20,000 enrollees, and one of my classes had 500 students in it," he said, reflecting on his preference for a more intimate learning environment as a self-proclaimed introvert.

Despite his initial enthusiasm for engineering, influenced by his love for tinkering and mechanics, he felt a growing disconnect with the rigid nature of the field.

This internal struggle, coupled with a longtime fascination for architecture, prompted John to consider the field—a blend of technical skill and artistic creativity that particularly appealed to his imaginative side.

Inspired by the iconic works of architects like Frank Lloyd Wright and Ludwig Mies van der Rohe, John recognized architecture as a potential career path.

His interest led him to apply to the Illinois Institute of Technology (now commonly known as Illinois Tech), renowned for its prestigious architecture program, and he was thrilled to be accepted.

John's decision to go to college marked a major turning point in his life, especially when he transferred to Illinois Tech. It was during his college years that he started to develop important skills like strategy, analysis, and foresight—skills that would later shape his career.

This time was about more than just getting good grades; it was about building a new identity that went beyond the expectations and usual paths from his early life. At Illinois Tech, surrounded by a world full of creative possibilities, switching his major was more than just a change in focus; it was a big step forward, opening up new challenges and opportunities for him to grow and explore.

As John pursued the new opportunities of college life, his mother had also taken practical steps by investing in a laundromat to help support the family financially. His aunts had also tried to run a laundromat on North Clark Street, but after they struggled to keep it afloat, the business fell into his mother's hands.

Initially, John's role was to maintain and repair the machines during his visits home from U of I, drawing on his mechanical skills honed from years of tinkering with cars. After John moved back to Chicago to attend Illinois Tech, his mother offered him the chance to take over the laundromats, believing that managing the business would provide him with valuable experience and responsibility.

John rapidly broadened his role from simple maintenance man to actively propelling the business forward. Seeing it a means to fund his college education, he looked for opportunities to expand, and his efforts paid off—he soon was overseeing three laundromats.

"Running those laundromats taught me as much about economics as any course I took in college," John remembered. He expanded the business by opening a facility in Cicero, a Chicago suburb, which combined dry cleaning services with traditional laundromat functions—the first of its kind in the area.

This venture was more than just a business operation; it was a practical education in entrepreneurship and strategic business management. As John considered buying another laundromat, the current owner showed him promising revenue figures.

However, John felt that something didn't quite add up. This experience became a lesson about the critical importance of due diligence and verification.

"I was trying to figure out if he was telling the truth," John recalled. The owner's claims were substantial, and the price of the business was based on these figures. To verify the accuracy of these claims, John requested something that wasn't usually scrutinized in such deals—the utility bills.

"I wanted to see how much electricity and utilities were actually being used," he explained. He knew from experience that the cost of utilities often mirrored a laundromat's activity level.

By comparing these utility bills to the revenue of his own stores, John discovered a significant discrepancy. "He was down about 50% from what he was telling me," John noted. The utility bills showed that the machines were running much less than the owner claimed, suggesting he had exaggerated his revenue figures.

This experience was an eye-opener for John, teaching him the value of doing his own thorough research. "It was teaching me to be careful, to investigate," he explains. It firmly set the foundation for John's approach to business: meticulous, curious, and always skeptical. These early lessons in scrutiny and the importance of solid evidence became pillars of his professional ethos.

In addition to funding his education, owning the laundromats enabled him to buy a 1963 Corvette—something he had always dreamed of. "I've always loved cars!" John said.

More important, the laundromats taught him the value of under-standing every aspect of a business and performing the due diligence to determine if an investment is truly as good as it sounds. These principles would significantly influence his business philosophy in the years to follow, emphasizing the necessity for hands-on management.

Chapter 4

Shaping His Vision

Although John transferred to Illinois Tech for its renowned architecture program, he soon discovered the campus also offered a more intimate and intellectually stimulating environment.

In the campus lounge, John often engaged in conversations with professors over coffee, discussing topics like philosophy, economics, and the historical events that shaped Western civilization. It was during these in-depth discussions that John's passion for deep thinking began to develop.

"I started getting into philosophy and history a lot more," John shared, his eyes lighting up as he recalled those days. "One of the things that really got me hooked was the Great Books of the Western World series. It was a collection of works from some of the greatest minds in Western thought, like Plato, Aristotle, Shakespeare, and Darwin.

"It wasn't just a collection of books—it was a doorway to new ways of thinking, filled with ideas that have shaped our understanding of the world. Those books opened my mind to a whole new level of perspective."

This exploration not only deepened his academic knowledge but also strengthened his connection to his Greek heritage, fostering a profound appreciation for its contributions to the world.

His conversations with professors weren't just about absorbing information; they were about shaping his ability to think critically and independently. "You don't go to school to learn what to think, but how to think," John often remarks, reflecting on his academic journey.

Studying philosophy, for John, was a deep dive into the practice of critical thinking. It involved constantly questioning, "How should we think about this? What should we be doing about this?" These sessions, rich with dialogue and debate, were fundamental in teaching him not just to accept information at face value but also to analyze and challenge it.

But it wasn't just the philosophers from long ago that caught John's attention. Milton Friedman, the famed economist of the era, also made a lasting impression on him. "Listening to Milton Friedman was something else," John said. "He taught economics in a way that tied it back to our freedoms, emphasizing that democracy is all about having the freedom to make choices."

This combination of historical knowledge and modern economic theory didn't just educate John; it helped him see the world differently. Influenced by professors and works like Milton and Rose Friedman's *Free to Choose*, John didn't just learn facts—he was learning to think about the broader implications of freedom and governance in new ways.

One of the most defining moments of John's early days at Illinois Tech, however, was an unexpected interview with none other than Ludwig Mies van der Rohe, then head of the architecture department. Mies van der Rohe was a German American architect—a giant in the field of modern architecture.

Known for pioneering the use of glass and steel in large office buildings, Mies van der Rohe's influence was profound and his presence at the school made the learning environment incredibly inspiring for John.

John's fascination with architecture was also deeply influenced by the distinct style of Frank Lloyd Wright. "Each architect's approach to design and the features they emphasized really made me think about what kind of architect I wanted to become," John explained.

Frank Lloyd Wright's Prairie style, known for its harmony with the environment, starkly contrasted Mies van der Rohe's sleek, modernist designs of glass and steel.

John found the distinct styles of each architect deeply influential, stating, "It was fascinating to see how each architect's signature style communicated different ideals and emotions."

John's engagement with these diverse architectural philosophies broadened his understanding of design. "Every design, every building tells a story," he mused. This exposure influenced his future personal and professional environments significantly; inspired by Frank Lloyd Wright's architecture, he built his first home in the Prairie style, and years later commissioned Dirk Lohan, Mies van der Rohe's grandson, to design the Calamos headquarters.

Although John had a passion for architecture, as his college career progressed, he decided to switch gears and focus on economics. "Economics impacts everything, and the more I learned, the more fascinated I became," he shared.

While studying at Illinois Tech, John watched President John F. Kennedy deliver his iconic inauguration speech, where he challenged Americans to shift their focus from what the country could do for them to what they could contribute to the country.

This message struck a chord with John, especially when linked to his philosophy classes where he encountered Socrates's vision of a well-lived life that progresses from student to soldier to statesman. This concept deeply resonated with John, igniting in him a firm sense of patriotism and duty to defend democracy.

John was further inspired by a poster he spotted in the Air Force ROTC building on campus. It depicted a pilot about to land on an aircraft carrier, captioned, "This is my office."

This image portrayed a sense of adventure and duty that resonated deeply with him, and he re-enlisted in Air Force ROTC. While John's first experience in ROTC had been to fulfill a requirement, a profound sense of purpose now drove his decision.

After graduating with his economics degree in 1963, John was commissioned as a second lieutenant and was slated for pilot training. However, his former finance professor opened up a new opportunity. "There's a new program called the MBA, or Master of Business Administration," his professor explained. "It's a graduate degree that prepares students to effectively lead and manage businesses," he added, recommending it as a valuable step for John's future.

Intrigued by the prospect of blending his military obligations with further education, John saw a chance to expand his horizons. He approached the ROTC with a crucial question: could he delay his active duty to pursue an advanced degree? When he received an affirmative response, it opened the door for him to enroll in the MBA program.

Over the next two years, John immersed himself in business and finance, developing skills that would form the backbone of his future career.

During his time at Illinois Tech, John's life outside the classroom was just as busy and shaping as his demanding studies. Although many students concentrated only on their coursework, John was also experiencing major life events.

Balancing school with his personal life was quite a challenge for John. As he worked toward his master's degree, he wasn't just a student—he was also a husband. Things became even busier in 1963 when he and his wife welcomed their first child, John Jr., proudly adding *father* to his list of responsibilities. "Becoming a dad was incredible," John said. "It made everything more meaningful."

As he was wrapping up his MBA, the Air Force called him to start his training, signaling the end of his time in academia and as an entrepreneur.

Facing imminent deployment and with no family member to take over, John was forced to quickly sell his laundromat business, which had not only financed his studies but also provided him with invaluable lessons in business management. The profits not only supported his family but also provided the financial backing necessary for his MBA studies.

"Selling those laundromats was bittersweet, but it helped me move forward at a crucial time," John reflected.

This chapter in John's life was marked by his entrepreneurial spirit and practical business skills, laying a strong foundation for his future endeavors. His university days were pivotal, where he honed his ability to tackle complex societal issues through philosophical inquiry and economic theory. These lessons profoundly shaped his perspective and continued to influence his responses to the world's evolving challenges.

Chapter 5

Active Duty

After putting his MBA studies on hold at Illinois Tech, John entered active duty with the Air Force where his military training expanded dramatically, adapting to the practical demands of his new role.

He embarked on a year-long pilot training program at Webb Air Force Base in Big Spring, Texas, that rigorously prepared him to handle high-performance jets. This segment of his officer training was not only about mastering the controls but also about embracing a disciplined approach to every aspect of flying. "It was very important to make sure you're doing your homework, you're checking everything," John emphasized, underscoring the significance of following detailed checklists, procedures, and protocols crucial for safe and effective operations.

John's pilot training was an intense and defining period in his life. The program demanded unwavering focus—a skill that was crucial not just for flying but for his future endeavors as well. The training was grueling; out of a class of 60 aspiring pilots, only half would successfully navigate the demands and graduate.

Early on, he struggled with severe nausea while flying, and the coursework was incredibly rigorous. There were many moments when he wondered if he was cut out to be a pilot. But his determination kept him going, and his perseverance paid off.

For John, earning his Air Force Wings wasn't just a professional achievement; it was a proud and memorable milestone that marked his transition from student to military aviator, imbuing him with a profound sense of accomplishment and readiness.

Additionally, John's leadership skills were honed through various team-building exercises, which were an integral part of his early training in ROTC and continued into his active duty. "We were always taught how to work together," he recalled, highlighting the focus on cooperation and leadership that were critical to his development as an officer.

After his specialized training in Merced, California, John was stationed at Beale Air Force Base (AFB), where he flew B-52s as part of the Strategic Air Command (SAC).

With his daughter Laura just born, John and his young family settled in Yuba City, California, north of Sacramento, not far from Beale AFB.

Originally established in 1942 as Camp Beale, the base underwent several transformations to support diverse military operations during World War II and its aftermath, adapting to meet evolving strategic needs.

By 1967, Beale AFB had become a crucial site for the US Air Force's SAC. The base itself was equipped with expansive runways, large hangars, and advanced maintenance facilities to accommodate the sophisticated aircraft.

The military community there included highly trained pilots, reconnaissance experts, engineers, and support staff, all dedicated to the strategic defense efforts of the United States.

Initially, John's assignment was to pilot B-52s on critical 24-hour missions from Beale AFB to the North Pole to await instructions, each aircraft armed with nuclear weapons as a Cold War deterrent. These missions served as continuous preparations for potential conflict, with the specter of World War III a constant presence.

Flying over the remote Arctic, John faced the profound responsibility of handling the powerful arsenal aboard. Each safe return to Beale AFB was a relief, underscoring the delicate balance between national defense and the potential for global catastrophe.

John decided to buy a house, aiming to provide a stable and comfortable home for his family away from the base. The decision not to live on base was driven by John's anticipation of a five-year duty period at Beale AFB. This seemed like a prudent choice, ensuring his family's comfort over the long term—but events on the other side of the world would change his plans.

The community in Yuba City, populated with other military families, provided a network of support and camaraderie that was crucial during this time of transition. Living off base enabled John to maintain a semblance of normal family life amid the demands of military service.

John expected to spend the next five years flying missions for the SAC out of Beale AFB. "I thought I'd be settled there, flying B-52s for a good long stretch," he recalled. However, John's career took an unexpected turn when he was reassigned to Vietnam, not to fly B-52s, but in a vastly different capacity. "It was a complete surprise," John admitted, finding himself designated as a Forward Air Controller (FAC), one of the military's more dangerous roles that placed him directly at the perilous nexus of aerial and ground operations in North Vietnam.

As a FAC, John took on the crucial and high-risk task of directing air strikes from a small, often slow-moving aircraft, the Cessna O-2 Skymaster, a military version of the Cessna 337 Super Skymaster.

Known as the *Oscar Deuce*, the O-2 was equipped with twin engines arranged in a pusher-tractor configuration, mounted under a high wing and flanked by twin tail booms. This design helped minimize the aerodynamic drag and provided a centerline thrust, enhancing its maneuverability and stability in flight.

Active Duty

Without FACs pinpointing enemy locations on the ground, "fast movers"—the fighter jets packed with bombs and other ordinance—had no way to effectively target the enemy attacking American troops in the field.

Despite the dangers, it was John's belief that if Uncle Sam wanted him to be a FAC, he would dedicate himself to the assignment and do it to the very best of his ability.

Deeply influenced by his family's patriotism for their adopted homeland and inspired by President John F. Kennedy's iconic call to service in his inaugural address, John felt a profound sense of duty to serve. "My solemn commitment not only influenced my military service," John says, "but would also continue to guide my life and career thereafter."

After training to fly the B-52, with its eight jet engines and capacity to carry up to 70,000 pounds of weaponry on missions of up to 8,800 miles, John was now tasked with flying the relatively small O-2 on nimble missions just above the jungle treetops. This shift represented a significant change in the spectrum of Air Force airframes, yet the O-2 played a vital role in the Vietnam conflict.

Its capabilities made the O-2 well-suited for observation, artillery spotting, and light attack missions, crucial for coordinating airstrikes and providing battlefield intelligence.

Most important, the O-2's ability to pinpoint targets for the fast movers significantly reduced the risk of friendly fire, when Air Force jets might accidentally strike American troops on the ground.

Equipped to direct heavily armed fighter and bomber aircraft to their targets, the O-2 carried white phosphorus rockets to mark these targets for attack. Fitted with additional radios and communication equipment, it facilitated coordination between ground forces and air assets. "I'd shoot a white phosphorus rocket to the ground, and I'd direct the jets to 'hit my smoke,'" John explained, describing their method for directing airstrikes.

This transition from high-altitude bomber missions to frontline aerial coordination was a significant shift for John, testing his adaptability and ability to manage the stresses and rapid decisions required in combat.

Given the new assignment, the complexity of John's training further increased with specialized jungle training in the Philippines, a preparatory course designed to equip him for the unpredictable conditions of Vietnam. Due to the dangers of his mission, not all of his training was behind the flight stick.

"We were on the ground, and the training was about getting from point A to point B without being caught," John explained. The exercises included evading so-called hunters—local personnel trained to search for and "capture" trainees.

"We had these little tabs, about six of them, and if we were caught, we had to surrender one as a penalty," John recalled, detailing the elements of the training.

The trainers used the dense jungle environment to their advantage, teaching John and his fellow trainees how to move stealthily and stay aware of their surroundings at all times.

"You'd be looking out for people who might be climbing in trees or walking through the trees. It was quite an experience," John added, reflecting on the intensity and uniqueness of the training.

This rigorous preparation was crucial for what lay ahead in Vietnam, where John's role as a FAC put him directly in harm's way. This combination of intense training and real-world application underscored John's adaptability and courage, traits that were continually tested throughout his service in the challenging and unpredictable conditions of the Vietnam War.

"Every day brought new challenges, but you learned to think on your feet quickly," John said, reflecting on the intense nature of his new role.

John landed in Vietnam shortly after the massive Tet Offensive, a major turning point in the Vietnam War that marked a series of coordinated surprise attacks by the North Vietnamese forces on scores of cities, towns, and military bases throughout South Vietnam.

This period of intense combat activity ensured that he and his colleagues in the 20th Tactical Air Support Squadron at Da Nang Air Base would be continually engaged.

Da Nang Air Base was a hive of military activity, serving as one of the busiest airports in the world at the time. It housed a mix of US fighter jets and helicopters and was crucial for launching air operations, making it a frequent target of enemy attacks.

John flew missions that were reactionary and on-call, based on the immediate needs of ground troops. "I might fly two missions a day," John described. "We might not have a specific mission when we took off, but as we circled our area, ground troops would call us for help."

Flying these missions required constant vigilance and adaptability. John learned to never fly straight and level to avoid enemy fire. "We were pretty low, so I always flew turning, making sure they couldn't get a shot at me," he explained.

Each successful return to the base at Da Nang was a relief, though sometimes John would learn of the dangers he had narrowly escaped only when the crew chief pointed out bullet holes in his aircraft.

John's service in Vietnam was marked by periods of sudden and intense combat, interspersed with days of deceptive calm. "One day it'd be nothing happening, the next day you're getting shot at," John described, capturing the unpredictable nature of his deployment.

One mission in particular underscored the heavy responsibilities and quick decision-making required in his role. John was tasked with leading an airstrike against what was reported as enemy soldiers in the water.

As he piloted his aircraft closer to the target for a better look, he realized it was actually a family fishing, not combatants. With little time to spare, John made the critical decision to call off the strike, saving civilian lives. "You've got to really trust what you're doing," he reflected, acknowledging the weight of each decision in such fraught situations.

This close call was a vivid reminder of the ethical dilemmas and the importance of precision in wartime actions. It also reignited John's spiritual life, which had waned since his college days. Facing daily life-and-death situations brought his faith back into sharp focus.

"Once I got to Vietnam, I remembered my faith and how important it was to pray every day," John shared, recalling how the old saying held true for him: "There are no atheists in foxholes."

These experiences deepened his spiritual reliance. Navigating through clouds and enemy fire, John found himself reaching out for divine protection, a practice that became a cornerstone of his resilience.

Chapter 6

Red Smoke!

On a bright, sunny day above the battle-scarred terrain of North Vietnam, 28-year-old Captain John Calamos piloted his Cessna O-2 Skymaster on yet another mission deep into enemy territory. The clear skies and vibrant sunlight belied the dark and imminent danger lurking below, where every shadow could conceal a threat, and every moment could turn deadly.

Flying above the dense jungle canopy, he raced toward his target, his nerves on edge, fully aware that at any moment, enemy anti-aircraft fire could erupt from the jungle floor to tear through his fragile Cessna O-2 aircraft.

At an altitude ranging between 1,000 and 1,500 feet, precision was challenging but essential, and John relied mostly on visual cues from the horizon and the jungle treetops to judge his position. His eyes continuously darted across his cockpit instruments: his altimeter, airspeed indicator, and fuel gauge—all critical. Their readings kept him informed and alive in this high-stakes environment.

The interior of the cockpit was sweltering despite the open vents. The Vietnamese climate, combined with the heat of the engines and the stress of combat, made it oppressively hot. Sweat trickled down John's forehead, his flight suit sticking uncomfortably to his skin.

His hands were clammy on the controls. The acrid smell of napalm, blended with the odors of oil and metal that filled the cockpit, served as a constant reminder of the dangers he faced.

The radio, his lifeline to the world beyond his cockpit, crackled with voices, coordinating movements for the impending airstrikes. He constantly switched among three radio channels, a juggling act of communication with ground forces, air support, and his base in Da Nang. Each frequency carried vital information, an amalgamation of updates, requests, and commands that guided his every decision.

As he flew over a particularly hot zone, the cockpit shook with the near-misses of ground fire. "That was a close one!" he muttered to himself. "Skymaster Two-One, watch your six! Tracer fire at your altitude!" a voice cautioned over the radio.

Operating close to enemy lines to accurately pinpoint targets, he faced constant threats from anti-aircraft fire, necessitating continual, agile maneuvering to avoid being hit.

Unlike most military aircraft that have some degree of armor and redundant systems to keep flying after being hit by the enemy, his little Cessna O-2 didn't offer much survivability. This demanding environment required John to maintain sharp focus, exceptional situational awareness, and a calm demeanor under pressure, all honing his ability to navigate risk—a skill that would become crucial to his success in future endeavors.

As he marked targets for the incoming jets, his voice was firm, directing the pilots with precision. "Skymaster Two-One, you're over the target area, adjust heading two-five-zero." The voice from Da Nang control was calm but urgent in his headset. "Roger that, adjusting now," John replied, his voice steady despite the adrenaline coursing through him.

As he banked his plane for a quick descent, he dropped a phosphorus rocket pinpointing the enemy. "Cleared in hot," he radioed, "your target is marked, I'm pulling up," ensuring his escape from the strike zone. As he ascended, the engine's hum climbed in pitch, and the glow from the explosions below flashed in the plane's windows.

Switching the radio to the ground force frequency, John coordinated with units under heavy attack. Amid the chaos of a fierce firefight, an urgent call broke through the static: "We need immediate support; they're all over us!" Despite the pandemonium of this mission—and every other—John felt a profound clarity.

Unsure of their exact position and to avoid friendly fire, John instructed the ground troops to use smoke signals—a common practice to visually convey location in such dire situations.

"Show me a green smoke," John ordered. But two green smoke plumes came up through the trees instead of one. That's when John realized the enemy was likely listening, having deciphered their signals and sending up smoke signals of its own.

John quickly adapted. "Show me white smoke," he instructed, and two plumes of white smoke appeared.

Then he requested a red smoke—a crucial test. When only a single puff of red smoke rose and the ground troop reported back, "We don't have red smoke," John immediately recognized the implications: the enemy had unwittingly revealed its location.

A knowing look crossed his face, and his eyes lit up with satisfaction. "Got 'em!" he whispered to himself. Confidently, he radioed the command, "The red smoke is your target. Cleared in hot!" as he authorized another decisive ground strike.

As the final moments of the day's mission ticked by, John's journey back to the base was accompanied not by relief but by the sobering realization that another day and another mission awaited.

Amid the rigors of his routine, he looked forward to unwinding at the officer's club, a gathering place where fellow Air Force and Navy pilots, Marines, and ground troops came together. They would

Red Smoke!

share drinks, shoot pool, play cards, and throw darts, enjoying each other's company and momentarily escaping the stresses of duty.

However, these moments of camaraderie contrasted sharply with the harrowing missions that pushed him to his limits, culminating in a perilous nighttime mission in September 1968, which would test him like never before.

Chapter 7

The Defining Mission

Over the course of the Vietnam War, John flew over 400 sorties, amassing 833 combat hours in tense skies over battlefields, with every enemy combatant aiming to shoot him down.

Each flight presented its own challenges, demanding a high level of vigilance and adaptability. "You learn to rely not just on your training but also on your instincts. You have to, when every mission could mean life or death," he said.

That was certainly the case on the evening of September 28, 1968, when Captain John Calamos took to the night sky under his call name, Lopez 58. John's mission that fateful night was directly tied to the broader strategic efforts that had begun three years earlier, when the Military Assistance Command Vietnam Studies and Observation Group initiated the establishment of Special Forces camps to bolster defenses along the Laotian border to counter North Vietnamese operations.

These crucial forward bases, including Camp A-109 at Thuong Duc, were operated by Special Forces A-Teams and the indigenous Montagnard paramilitaries they trained into an effective fighting force. The camp at Thuong Duc was advantageously situated between two ridges for tactical superiority, providing a clear view over the river valley for monitoring enemy movements and defense. It was also an operational hub for the 5th Special Forces Group, which actively monitored North Vietnamese Army (NVA) activity.

The main compound of Camp A-109 was secured at the center, surrounded by a sophisticated network of communication lines and rapid response routes that connected to a series of outer Montagnard-operated camps and outposts. This setup not only facilitated efficient command and control but also enabled swift countermeasures against any attempted infiltration or assault by enemy forces.

However, given its critical location on one of the NVA's key infiltration routes, the camp was inevitably a prime target for North Vietnamese forces. Thuong Duc was located approximately 25 miles southwest of Da Nang Air Base, the primary station for John and his fellow Forward Air Controllers (FACs), enhancing its logistical and operational capabilities.

The FACs of the United States Air Force, along with their counterparts in the Army, Marines, and Navy, represent one of the lesser-known yet significant narratives of the Vietnam War. Originating from roles established during the First World War, FACs had been active in Vietnam since 1962.

These pilots, flying solo, undertook a range of responsibilities including gathering intelligence on NVA troop movements, arms, and strength, serving as vital communication links between ground and air forces, and notably, orchestrating combat search-and-rescue operations.

Whenever Special Forces, Marines, or Army units required support from the air, it was the FAC who would pilot their compact Cessna O-2 Skymaster into the battle zones.

The FAC held the authority to call in air strikes on enemy positions and could redirect air assets from other missions if ground units were at risk of being overrun by NVA forces. These controllers were always on standby, ready to respond wherever needed.

Understandably, FACs in their small, unarmored Cessna O-2s were vigilant about avoiding anti-aircraft fire, and the risk of capture if shot down. "We tried to stay clear of ground fire," John explained, "Keeping above 1,500 feet and avoiding flying straight and level for extended periods was crucial. Ground fire was frequent, including from small arms. When launching rockets, we had to drop altitude to ensure accuracy, but we quickly ascended back to 1,500 feet."

The O-2's slow cruising speed of about 140 to 150 knots allowed it to "loiter" effectively over localized battles, which was crucial for maintaining oversight of ground developments. By contrast, the faster McDonnell F-4 Phantoms and North American F-100 Super Sabres were less effective in close air support when combatants were separated by only a few hundred yards or shrouded by dense jungle foliage. Achieving pinpoint accuracy was essential for safeguarding American and Allied forces.

John saw the importance of this firsthand during his assignments around Qua Nam, including the Thuong Duc camp. "There were about six of us at Da Nang," he recalled. "Our sectors covered areas where close air support was critical." The NVA were relentless in their efforts to disrupt American and Allied operations, and Camp A-109 quickly became a major point of contention.

As the war progressed, the strategic importance of the camp at Thuong Duc only grew, underscoring the ongoing and intense conflict that defined this volatile region. It was against this backdrop of heightened danger and critical military operations that John would perform acts of valor, highlighting his bravery and skill in one of Vietnam's most fraught theaters of war.

Beginning in mid-September 1968, in a covert operation, two NVA infantry regiments, totaling about 3,000 soldiers, stealthily positioned mortars and artillery to encircle the camp at Thuong Duc and its outposts from three sides. The full-scale assault on Camp A-109 was launched at 2:00 a.m. on September 28, when forces from the NVA's 21st and 141st Regiments quickly overtook Outposts Alpha and Bravo, situated 600 yards from the camp's perimeter.

Throughout the day, Green Berets and Camp Strikers had mounted successful counterattacks to reclaim the crucial outposts. Enemy forces countered with intensified assaults, bombarding nearby villages with mortar and artillery to focus heavier fire on the camp.

Despite the escalating aggression, the Special Forces and Montagnards fiercely fought off the attacks. However, as darkness descended, the conflict was far from over.

That's when Captain Calamos was brought in to take over from the FAC who had coordinated air strikes throughout the day.

The darkness was both helpful and hindering. For John in his compact Cessna O-2, it meant constantly scanning the ground for the flashes of gunfire, tracers, and explosions.

"Tracers heading my way. I can't see NVA, but the ground fire tells me exactly where they are," John relayed urgently over the radio.

His updates primarily came from the Green Berets on the ground. "Just got word—the enemy is only two hundred feet away from our guys," John communicated, stressing the proximity. "They're too close; the jets can't drop their loads safely."

Realizing the critical need for better visibility, John coordinated with the air base. "We need flares now—more light to sort them out," he insisted. Soon, other planes responded by dropping flares, shedding continuous streams of stark, eerie white light that transformed the night into day across the battlefield, revealing the hidden movements below.

John urgently contacted Da Nang for backup, his voice tense over the radio. "We need more Phantoms and Super Sabres here with full loads. It's getting heavy down there."

As the jets swooped in low, releasing cluster munitions and general-purpose bombs, John's O-2 shook intensely from the shockwaves.

The explosions lit up the night sky in dazzling bursts of yellow and white, momentarily blinding him.

Below, the small fires that erupted added a gruesome glow to the battlefield, illuminating the chaos, casualties, and abandoned weaponry.

Despite the devastation, the two NVA regiments continued their relentless advance, searching for any weakness in the American and Montagnard lines. Their movements, however, did not escape John's watchful eye.

"Enemy's still pushing," John reported, his voice firm yet calm. "Prepping for another strike."

Recognizing the stubborn resolve of the enemy, John coordinated another full air assault. "Load up, coming in again!" he directed as he marked the targets with white phosphorus rockets. "Cleared in hot!" John's command echoed over the radio, setting the stage for another round of intense bombardment. "The second strike came in and hit right where I had put my rockets," John said.

In addition to the jets, John's call brought in a formidable AC-47 gunship, affectionately known as *Spooky* and *Puff the Magic Dragon*, which showcased its extraordinary aerial firepower as it entered the fray.

This modified C-47 transport was outfitted with three 7.62 mm General Electric rotary miniguns, each with six rotating barrels akin to a Gatling gun and capable of firing 2,000–6,000 rounds per minute from a 5,000-round belt.

Typically loaded with a combat reserve of 24,000 rounds, the pilot used crosshairs on the left-side window to target. The AC-47 performed a counter-clockwise "pylon turn" to keep a continuous, cone-shaped barrage of bullets over a football field–sized area.

Enhanced by the night's glowing tracers that resembled orange laser beams, this targeting was further facilitated by visible ground fire and mortar explosions. The gunship's relentless bullet stream tore through the jungle, wreaking havoc and inflicting heavy casualties on the NVA forces.

After four solid hours flying over the fight and calling in every air asset that could be of help, John was relieved and flew back to Da Nang.

The camp was secured later that day when two battalions of the 7th Marines came in and drove the NVA back bringing closure to a fierce battle that resulted in significant casualties for the NVA.

The FACs and Air Force were critical in keeping the camp and surrounding area secure. However, it was Captain John Calamos's overnight mission that proved decisive, turning the tide in favor of the defenders with his heroic performance throughout the night.

His story is a vivid chapter in the annals of the Air Force's FACs, whose bravery and skill under pressure saved countless lives.

President Richard Nixon awarded John the Distinguished Flying Cross for his heroic actions, a recognition that spoke to his courage, skill, and dedication. The citation highlighted his "extraordinary achievement," a testament to his crucial role in ensuring the survival of the Special Forces camp against overwhelming odds.

* * *

The President of the United States takes great pleasure in presenting the Distinguished Flying Cross to Captain John P. Calamos for extraordinary achievement while participating in aerial flight as a Forward Air Controller near Thuong Duc Special Forces Camp in Southeast Asia on 28 September 1968. On that date, Captain Calamos flew in support of the Special Forces camp which was under heavy hostile attack. In spite of darkness, marginal weather conditions and poor visibility, Captain Calamos directed two sets of fighter aircraft, one flare aircraft, and one "Spooky" gunship against the hostile forces. Throughout the four hour mission, hostile forces continuously fired at his aircraft. Due to his outstanding airmanship, the camp was later relieved of the hostile pressure. The professional competence, aerial skill, and devotion to duty displayed by Captain Calamos reflect great credit upon himself and the United States Air Force.

Chapter 8

Back to the States

In May of 1969, as John's deployment in Vietnam neared its conclusion, he received the long-awaited and much-welcomed orders that he would be rotating back to the States. "I remember the profound sense of relief I felt knowing I was going home," John recalled.

His family were grateful and relieved to have John back home, yet beyond their household, the prevailing tension of the era was palpable. "It was a strange time," John reflected on his return, his voice heavy with the memory.

The Vietnam War had sharply divided the American public, with many turning their disdain toward the returning veterans instead of focusing on the government that sent them to Vietnam. "They advised us not to wear our uniforms in public, even on the flight back. There was real resistance to the war, and it affected those of us coming home," he recounted.

Rather than warm welcomes or expressions of gratitude, John received only quiet acknowledgments. "No one really said, 'Thanks for your service.' It wasn't like that at all," he shared.

John hoped to settle into a quieter phase of his military career, ideally spending the remaining year and a half of his service at Beale Air Force Base, in California flying B-52s—a role he felt suited for given his extensive combat experience.

49

However, his plans were abruptly changed by new orders from the Air Force. Instead of a tranquil stint in California, he was assigned to Minot, North Dakota, known for its isolated location and harsh weather conditions. "The irony wasn't lost on me," John said with a wry smile. "From the sunny coasts of California to the frigid plains of North Dakota—why not, right?"

The move required quick adjustments; he had to sell his house, uproot his family, and relocate to a place that was starkly different from sunny California or bustling Chicago.

Adjusting to life in North Dakota was a steep learning curve for John and his family. "Getting the family settled in was tough at first. Everything was so different, the weather, the people, the pace of life," John recounted.

On arriving at Minot, John's first impression of the base reflected its stark isolation. "It was really out in the farmland, pretty isolated," he described.

Unlike other bases where he might have bought a home, he chose a different approach in Minot due to its remote location and his transient expectations. "I just rented a place there for the family. Didn't buy a house," he explained, emphasizing the temporary nature of his stay.

Minot Air Force Base (AFB) was, and still is, a challenging yet strategically significant posting for Air Force personnel. Winters can be frigid and harsh with temperatures averaging between 15 °F and −2 °F. But despite the difficult conditions, John's temporary home was of vital importance to America's defense.

Minot AFB was one of the bases under the Strategic Air Command (SAC), and home to the B-52 Stratofortress fleet, which played a critical role in the deterrence strategy during the Cold War. These aircraft were capable of carrying nuclear and conventional weapons. The base was also involved in managing Minuteman III intercontinental ballistic missiles, which were housed in underground silos scattered throughout the surrounding areas.

John continued in the same role he had at Beale AFB, piloting B-52 bombers for the SAC. He and his fellow pilots contributed significantly to the readiness and capability of the SAC. "Flying the B-52s there meant we were at the heart of America's aerial might during the Cold War," he explained.

"We were always on alert. That meant preparing the airplane for immediate takeoff and then waiting—just sitting in the alert bunker," he recounted. The airmen passed the time playing cards or watching TV, always maintaining a state of readiness.

John's experience at Minot AFB was marked by one particularly intense incident that illustrated the ever-present tension of the Cold War. It happened unexpectedly, in the deep quiet of an early morning.

"They told us if the klaxon rang, it was the real thing. We were to take off immediately," John recalled, capturing the gravity and suddenness of such alerts that defined the ever-present tension of strategic air defense.

"The quiet of the night was shattered at four in the morning when the alert klaxon blared," John recounted. "We were all asleep, and suddenly, we had to scramble for an immediate takeoff."

In a matter of moments, the base sprung to life as everyone rushed to their positions. "We had the planes ready to go at all times—fully loaded, fueled up. So, when that klaxon sounded, we all ran out to jump into the planes."

Within minutes, John and his crew were airborne, part of a squadron of six B-52s taking off at 30-second intervals. "As we climbed into the sky, all I could think was, 'Are we heading to Russia? Are we actually going to drop these bombs?'" John said, reflecting the gravity of their potential mission. They were carrying nuclear weapons, and the stakes couldn't be higher.

"As we flew north, the tension was palpable. We were all wondering if this was it—the moment we'd go from training to actual combat," he continued. But after some tense minutes that felt much longer, the order came through the radio: "Turn around, you're clear to go back home."

It turned out to be a false alert. "Later, we found out there was a mix-up back at the base—someone had pressed the wrong button," John explained, still amazed by the mistake. "It was a stark reminder of how close we were to a real conflict. Just a button between peace and potentially starting a war."

Luckily for all, the Cold War stayed cold that day.

John's transition from the Vietnam War battlefields to the tense atmosphere of the Cold War skies exemplifies the complex challenges veterans face when adapting to life after service. His experiences, deeply etched by moments where global peace seemed to hang by a thread and personal survival was a daily battle, highlighted the perpetual brinkmanship of the era.

"Each mission shaped me, showing how fragile peace can be and the heavy responsibility on those of us ready to defend it," John reflected introspectively on the profound effects of his active duty.

John came back to an America that didn't fully recognize what veterans like him had gone through. He felt fortunate to have survived his combat experience both physically and mentally intact, while so many of those he served alongside suffered from wounds both seen and unseen—including posttraumatic stress disorder, which the medical establishment was just beginning to understand.

Armed with the newfound strength he built from his years in service, John thought about the next chapter of his life as his remaining months of military service dwindled down. He considered becoming a commercial pilot, a natural and lucrative extension of his military flying career. But like so many times in John's life, the universe had different plans for him.

Chapter 9

Civilian Life Again

As his discharge date from active duty service drew near, John began seriously considering his next steps.

He weighed the option of leaving the military life completely to transition to civilian pursuits, and his discussions with fellow pilots sparked an interest in continuing to fly, albeit in a different capacity. "I talked a lot with other pilots; some of them were already flying with airlines, and that seemed like a logical next step for me," John explained.

The transition from military to commercial aviation was an increasingly common path among his peers. "There was always this ongoing discussion about which airline to join, what moves to make next," he said, reflecting on the camaraderie and shared aspirations among the pilots.

John's decision to pursue a career with an airline led him to Delta Air Lines. "They actually sent me tickets to fly out to Atlanta for an interview, straight from Minot," he recalled.

"They asked about my educational background. I mentioned my college and graduate school experience—and, of course, my flight hours," John explained. "Clearly, my experience of piloting a large aircraft like the B-52 was a positive for them," he noted.

He was glad the interviewers didn't seem offput by his service in Vietnam, a relief given the mixed sentiments toward the war back home. After the interview, John returned to Minot, still on active duty, and awaited the airline's decision. "They told me I qualified and that they'd let me know," he said, reflecting on the uncertain waiting period. "They didn't specify when they'd get back to me—could be a month, two months. They just confirmed I was in the running for the next training class."

The waiting was tense. "You can imagine, wanting that job, knowing you're qualified, but not knowing when they'll call—it was nerve-wracking," John admitted. Despite the uncertainty, he held onto hope as he returned to civilian life in Chicago, awaiting the call that would start his new career path with Delta.

After arriving back in Illinois, John and his young family initially lived with his brother Angelo's family while he searched for a home. He eventually bought a small house in the Chicago western suburb of Hinsdale, attracted by the quality schools for his kids. "I was looking for a good, safe place for my family, and Hinsdale seemed perfect," John explained.

During this transitional period, John also focused on completing his education. "I needed to finish just one course to get my MBA from Illinois Tech," he shared. In 1970, he successfully completed that course, marking a significant personal achievement. "It felt great to finally finish my MBA. It was something that had been hanging over me for years," he said.

However, John's plans to join the airline industry were derailed by the economic downturn in 1970, which led to the cancellation of the training class he was set to attend. "So, I had to think about what to do next," John recalled.

Despite this setback, his passion for aviation remained strong. "In 1970, after my discharge from active duty, I didn't want to give up flying, so I joined the Reserves," he shared, emphasizing his continued dedication to aviation.

He chose to join the 45th Tactical Fighter Squadron located at Grissom Air Force Base in neighboring Indiana for his service, situated about 150 miles from his home in Hinsdale.

In 1970, Grissom was a bustling center of military operations, known for its strategic importance and technological advancements. It was undergoing significant expansion, including the introduction of new aircraft such as the A-37 Dragonfly attack aircraft. "I was fortunate to be among the first to train on the A-37s there," John recalled with evident excitement.

"The thrill of flying a jet fighter was just incredible. Whether it was training in flight formation or refueling in the air, every moment was exhilarating," John shared.

This sense of exhilaration and challenge would continue to shape John's career, which has always been driven by a desire for expertise. He balanced his passion for both finance and aviation, using the sharp analytical skills and discipline he developed in the military to give him a unique edge when tackling the volatile financial markets of the 1970s.

Finance had always fascinated him—ever since he found stock certificates in the basement of his family's grocery store. Even while serving in the Reserves, he made time to study the markets and dive into financial literature.

His interest in convertible bonds, a unique investment tool that combines elements of both bonds and stocks, was sparked by the book *Beat the Market* by Edward O. Thorp, which introduced him to warrants, options, and convertible securities. John developed a fascination with convertible bonds.

He likened managing convertible bonds to flying an airplane, emphasizing the need to precisely navigate the opportunities and risks of both the stock and bond characteristics. "Just as in flying, managing risk is crucial," he noted, drawing a parallel between the careful risk assessment required in both aviation and finance.

John believed that convertible bonds offered a strategic investment choice for those looking to balance risk and reward, enabling participation in a company's potential upside with less risk than buying the stock outright. This comparison highlights the strategic complexity of convertible bonds and connects his technical and aviation skills with his financial acumen.

When John's plans with the airlines didn't take off, he pivoted to the financial sector, steering his career from the runways to the financial markets.

But John couldn't have picked a more challenging time to enter the financial services business. The early 1970s was a period of severe economic turmoil in the United States marked by stagflation—a perplexing mix of high inflation and stagnant growth. This harsh economic climate was worsened by the 1973 oil crisis, which quadrupled oil prices, led to energy shortages, and drove up the cost of goods.

Despite the faltering stock market and widespread economic uncertainty, John, who had a knack for spotting opportunity in adversity, applied to DuPont Glore Forgan, a Chicago firm that was actively hiring veterans.

John's interest in convertible bonds transformed from a casual curiosity into a professional specialty. "I really dug into them, and when I became a stockbroker, I used convertibles all the time," he explained. His focus was distinctive in the field where convertible bonds were often overlooked as complex and niche, setting him apart as an expert in a largely untapped area.

Navigating the fluctuating landscapes of the financial sector during the early 1970s proved challenging for John. He moved from one company to the next, primarily due to their instability or closure. "Some of the companies were getting into trouble and going out of business," John explained.

His expertise in convertible bonds set him apart, and he became a sought-after speaker and educator on the topic. "I even taught a course at a college in downtown Chicago about convertibles," he added.

John's frustration with the larger firms grew, especially when they tried to dictate his dealings with clients. "These big companies wanted to tell me what to buy and sell for my clients, which didn't sit right with me," John recalled, "I wanted to be free to give my clients solutions I really believed in."

John's career trajectory took a decisive turn following a particularly successful speech he gave on options trading. This event not only showcased his expertise but also underscored his growing dissatisfaction with the limitations placed on him by his then-employer. "I asked to give a speech to prospective clients focusing on how to use options effectively. The turnout was terrific, and it led to a lot of client calls and account openings," John said.

However, the response from his firm's management was not as encouraging as he had hoped.

After the success of his speech, John expressed his desire to repeat the performance, only to be informed that it would be a long while before he would have another opportunity. "They told me I could do it again in maybe two years. The guy in the corner office, he's going to do it next," John explained.

Frustrated, and seeing the potential to do more on his own, John made a swift decision. "I said, 'Okay, thank you very much. I'm leaving.'"

This led him and a small group of like-minded colleagues, including Tom Noddings, to take charge of their professional futures.

In 1977, they established their own firm, Noddings, Calamos & Associates, securing the autonomy they sought in their financial practices—a significant milestone in John's professional journey.

As he ventured into building his business, this blend of skills promised to guide him through the complexities of entrepreneurship and market fluctuations, setting the stage for the next chapter of his professional journey.

Chapter 10

Founding of Calamos Investments

John navigated an intense period of commitments throughout the 1970s, balancing his time between flying as a reservist, managing the responsibilities of fatherhood, and building his burgeoning career in financial services.

Twice a month, he'd be up in the air, piloting for the Air Force Reserves at Grissom Air Force Base. "I flew a lot, and it was tough, but the training was necessary," John admitted. Juggling his duties as a reservist with his responsibilities at home and his demanding job was no small feat.

During this time, John was promoted to major—a significant milestone that not only recognized his unwavering dedication but also honored the leadership and expertise he had cultivated over the years.

John's growing proficiencies in options trading coincided nicely with the founding of the Chicago Board Options Exchange (CBOE) in 1973, establishing him as a leading authority in the field and enhancing his expertise in convertible bonds.

This was the time when John began carving out his niche as a pioneering figure. He quickly became a prominent speaker, sharing his expertise on options trading with eager audiences, and a prolific writer, contributing to financial journals.

John caught the attention of Terry Savage, a trailblazer herself as a founding member and the first woman trader at the CBOE. Terry also hosted a financial news show from a small TV studio on the 41st floor of the Chicago Board of Trade building. The show known as *The Stock Market Observer* was broadcast on Channel 26, an ultrahigh frequency station before the widespread adoption of cable.

From the modest studio equipped with just two cameras and minimal staff, Terry conducted in-depth interviews from 1:00 p.m. to 2:00 p.m., dissecting complex market phenomena and exploring new financial instruments. It was here, amid the broadcast hours dedicated to stock market analysis, that John became a regular feature, sharing his expertise on convertible bonds and options trading.

Terry appreciated John's knack for simplifying complex financial topics. "John has a unique ability to break down sophisticated investment strategies like options trading and convertibles into understandable terms," Terry noted. "Our viewers really appreciated how he made such intricate subjects accessible and practical."

Through this experience, John recognized that media appearances, much like his speaking engagements, were valuable opportunities to educate potential clients and broaden his customer base. "After each show, I'd return to the office eager to see how many calls we received. It was a direct measure of our outreach's effectiveness," he noted.

He saw each interview as a chance to demystify complex financial concepts and connect with a wider audience. Making himself available to the media became an integral part of his marketing strategy moving forward. "My main goal was to help people understand the markets and manage risk effectively."

This approach was particularly relevant against the backdrop of the 1970s extreme market volatility and harsh economic conditions. It underscored why John vigorously advocated for the use of convertible bonds as a critical risk-management tool. As he navigated the complexities of establishing the new firm, he was joined by a small but dedicated team of about half a dozen colleagues.

The initial stages were financially challenging; John had to put everything he owned on the line, including leveraging his home to secure a mortgage to bring the startup to life. Despite the risks, the firm began to gain traction, attracting a diverse clientele and expanding its operations.

John detailed a typical day's rhythm: "I'd catch the early train, using that time to pore over the *Wall Street Journal* and prepare for the day ahead."

He would arrive at the office by eight, ready to dive into a packed schedule of research, client meetings, and strategy sessions. "It was a demanding routine, but incredibly fulfilling," he shared, painting a picture of a professional life driven by dedication and a deep commitment to his clients' success.

His approach was hands-on, preferring to react to the market's ebb and flow throughout the day rather than solely preparing in advance during the evenings. This dynamic work environment highlighted differences in business philosophy between John and his then-partner. "We had our own specialties and focuses, which initially worked well," John noted, but underlying tensions were present due to differing visions for the firm's future.

One day, John stumbled on an opportunity that would underscore their differences and significantly shape his future. He read about innovative investment strategies in an institutional investor magazine, particularly a piece on Delta Air Lines' pension fund's openness to new ideas.

Inspired, John drafted a detailed proposal on how convertible bonds could benefit Delta's pension strategy and mailed it to the fund's managers. This initiative led to Delta conducting a thorough due diligence of John's operations. Impressed with his expertise and the potential of convertible bonds, Delta hired John's firm to manage a portion of its pension fund's investments.

Although this arrangement meant earning fees rather than commissions, John saw it as an opportunity to expand his business and further specialize in convertible bonds. Reflecting on this unexpected turn, John remarked, "I once dreamed of flying for Delta, but instead I ended up managing a portion of their finances," emphasizing how his former aviation ambitions unexpectedly merged with his career in finance.

This initiative marked a significant turning point, making Delta his first institutional client—a relationship that lasted nearly 30 years despite his partner's skepticism. "He thought it was crazy, focusing on a low-commission client like that," John recounted. His partner preferred focusing on individual investors and had little interest in institutional clients, which contrasted with John's broader vision. These divergent paths eventually led to the firm splitting.

When the time came to divide the original firm, John reached a defining moment in his entrepreneurial journey. The breakup led to the founding of Calamos Financial Services, with a new base of operation in suburban Oak Brook, Illinois. Offering every team member a choice, many aligned with John, as a testament to their trust in his leadership and belief in his vision.

Up to this point, flying with the A-37 Reserve squadron had been a significant part of his life. Despite his busy schedule, John consistently managed to fit in essential reading and market research between flights during his weekends at Grissom AFB, ensuring he remained sharp and informed for his professional pursuits.

Fellow reservist Wendell Green fondly recalled how John used every spare moment to further his knowledge during their time in the Reserves. "Oh, yeah, I saw him," Wendell remarked when asked if he noticed John's unusual habit of burying himself in financial books between flights. "While most of us were unwinding or just chatting about routine stuff, John was always studying, staying on top of the financial world."

But John faced a pivotal decision when his squadron transitioned to the A-10 Thunderbolt II, which required several months of intensive training.

This new commitment clashed with the demands of his rapidly growing company. "I couldn't afford to step away for three to four months to train on a new airplane," John explained, highlighting the direct conflict between his military duties and business responsibilities.

By this time, John had dedicated nearly two decades to the military, starting with five years of active service that he regarded as his solemn duty to his country. This was followed by 12 years in the Reserves, when he balanced his military obligations and family responsibilities with his education and the escalating demands of a growing business.

His military career had shaped his identity profoundly, embedding a sense of duty and resilience into his character. But he knew what he had to do. Therefore, his decision to retire from the Reserves was not just a career change but a deeply personal and heart-wrenching choice. It marked a significant turning point, compelling John to fully commit to his business, while closing a chapter defined by dedication and sacrifice.

This decision was especially tough for John because he wasn't just leaving the squadron; he believed he'd be leaving behind the deep camaraderie he had found there. To John, the squadron was more than just a military unit; it was a brotherhood, similar to the bonds he formed with the Forward Air Controllers in Vietnam.

He was pleasantly surprised that many of his fellow Reservists, including Wendell, remained connected by becoming his first wealth management clients. Wendell once remarked, "I trusted John Calamos with my money because I trusted him with my life."

These bonds have stood the test of time, as John and his squadron friends continue to meet every January—just "the boys,"—to reminisce and strengthen their ties. Their annual reunions are more than social gatherings; they reaffirm a shared past that deeply resonates with each of them, underscoring the profound camaraderie that made John's decision to leave the Reserves so difficult.

His combination of entrepreneurial drive, expert knowledge, and a commitment to education helped John successfully navigate the early years of Calamos Financial Services.

His risk-managed and client-centric approach not only cemented the firm's reputation in the financial services industry but also solidified his standing as a respected leader and innovator.

Chapter 11

We Hired PhDs

As he was ramping up his own firm, John sought investment strategies that could thrive under uncertainty. The broader financial market, primarily comprising US stocks and bonds, was experiencing significant strain under the weight of high interest rates, rampant inflation, and a backdrop filled with political and geopolitical uncertainties.

"Convertibles did very well back then," he reflected. "But they weren't well known, and recognizing the opportunities of convertibles put us ahead of the investment banks and research companies. There wasn't even a dedicated convertible index at that time." Spurred by his success, John spearheaded the launch of his firm's first open-ended mutual fund for convertible bonds in 1985. "It was a groundbreaking step in the industry," John said with a note of pride.

John was proactive in promoting the new mutual fund. "I presented a lot, got invited by companies like Merrill Lynch, and we hired salespeople to help us expand," he said.

This period was not just about growth for Calamos Investments; it was about strategically responding to the market environment. "We weren't just trying to get big. It was about finding strategies that reflected the current market dynamics," he added.

As the decade progressed, John continued to innovate, launching additional funds that leveraged his expertise in convertibles to offer novel investment opportunities. In 1988, the firm introduced a fund that blended stocks and convertibles to provide risk-managed market participation, catering to investors seeking both growth and income in volatile markets.

John further expanded the fund lineup in 1990 with the launch of the firm's first fund dedicated to stocks. That same year, Calamos introduced its first liquid alternative mutual fund—a market-neutral offering that built on his expertise in convertible bond arbitrage.

"The fund primarily focused on earning income from convertible bonds while managing volatility by shorting the stock into which the bonds could convert," John detailed. This strategy not only demonstrated the versatile applications of convertibles but also marked a significant evolution in the firm's approach to offering comprehensive, risk-adjusted investment solutions.

"I believed that the mutual fund format would better suit our client base, which was largely composed of individual investors," he stated.

In launching the market-neutral fund, Calamos offered individual investors access to strategies typically reserved for institutional investors. This move was one that democratized advanced investment opportunities, bridging the gap between individual and institutional investors and showcasing his commitment to broadening access to sophisticated financial strategies.

The complexity of these financial instruments made promoting their benefits a challenging proposition in an era with limited information channels. Without the convenience of modern resources like specialized financial networks or internet searches, financial professionals had to rely heavily on direct communication and manual research to educate and sell these products.

"Back then, there wasn't much media coverage on business and financial markets like there is now. You had to really pick and choose, and do it manually," John explained. The labor-intensive nature of managing these investments contrasted sharply with the modern approaches of using preset models.

"During this period, our teamwork was invaluable. Our research team and trading desk stayed in constant communication, working side by side and sharing real-time updates on what was happening in the markets," John said.

This emphasis on communication also shaped John's approach to working with clients, ensuring they were always informed and involved.

Every client's distinct needs made personalized communication essential. "Every client I had was different," John emphasized, highlighting the necessity of tailoring explanations and education to individual goals and situations.

This bespoke approach was deeply influenced by his early experiences in customer service at his family's grocery store, where he learned the value of hard work and personalized attention. "That work ethic and the need to connect with each customer personally—those lessons from the grocery store were invaluable," he concluded.

Additionally, John recognized the critical importance of preserving capital, aware that his clients were entrusting him not only with their money but also with their financial security and the pursuit of their American Dreams. This understanding shaped his investment philosophy to focus on risk-managed strategies that prioritized long-term stability over short-term gains, reflecting the deep responsibility he felt toward each client's aspirations and financial well-being.

On Monday, October 19, 1987, known as Black Monday, the world faced a severe and unexpected stock market crash; this was the first major test for John and his firm. "It was a challenging day, to say the least," John recalled, reflecting on the chaos of that day as their phone lines were inundated with calls from anxious clients.

One couple, in particular, arrived at the office visibly distraught and near tears, convinced they had lost everything. In an era before clients had real-time access to their financial accounts, the uncertainty and fear were palpable.

But John was able to provide not just reassurance, but unexpectedly good news: their portfolio had withstood the turmoil, and they were still on track to meet their goals.

This moment underscored the significance of John's role and the deep responsibility he felt in safeguarding his clients' financial futures. It was a poignant reminder of how vital his guidance was in navigating the turbulent waters of financial markets, protecting not just investments, but the hopes and dreams of the families he served.

He highlighted his firm's resilience, emphasizing, "Our approach has always been about adapting to the market environment we find ourselves in." This adaptability proved crucial during the late 1980s and early 1990s as his firm developed strategies to both cope with and capitalize on volatile market conditions.

John credited his college education for fostering critical thinking, influenced by the great books of Western civilization and economist Milton Friedman's teachings. Friedman's perspective that economics is fundamentally about how a country is organized, and the essential freedom to choose deeply shaped John's economic views.

This foundation in critical thinking and economic freedom played a significant role in how John approached his business and his pursuit of the American Dream, viewing the country as an environment ripe for innovation. "That part of my education was crucial, not just during my college years but throughout my life, continually influencing how I think," John stated.

His admiration for Ronald Reagan also intertwined with his business philosophy, particularly in the context of Reagan's support for supply-side economics and reduced governmental interference in business. "I admired Reagan's perspective that the government should act as a referee, not trying to manage everything but ensuring fair play," John noted, reflecting on how this influenced his views as an investor and business owner.

Reagan's speeches, particularly those supporting Barry Goldwater, resonated with John because of their alignment with Friedman's principles. "Reagan's approach to economics and governance reminded me of Friedman's advocacy for free choice and minimal government," he said, acknowledging the profound impact these two figures had on shaping his approach to business and investment.

John's recruitment strategies focused on observing potential hires in action to ensure they fit the company's culture of proactive problem-solving and adaptability. "In those early days, I realized how important it was to see candidates in action, not just in interviews," John explained.

He pioneered an internship program that welcomed students from his alma mater Illinois Tech. This initiative served not only to give students valuable experience but also as a crucial evaluation tool. "It's difficult to truly understand someone from just an hour-long interview. Our internship program allowed us to gauge how they would contribute to our team over time," he noted.

John was particular about the qualities he looked for in his team, emphasizing the need for determination and a strong work ethic, qualities he summed up with a phrase he had picked up: "We hire PhDs—poor, hungry, and determined." This approach helped him identify individuals who were not just skilled but also passionately driven, mirroring the ethos he wanted to embed within Calamos Investments.

On the philosophical front, John aimed to instill a culture that was deeply aligned with his business values. "I didn't have a formal booklet outlining our culture in those early days, but I was very clear about hiring the right people for the right roles," he mentioned.

This included ensuring that each team member, whether in investments, accounting, legal, or client relations, not only had the necessary skills but also shared the company's core motivations. Key among these motivations were being team players, a trait John deeply valued from his time in the military, which emphasized collaboration and collective effort.

He also prioritized a client-first mentality, reminiscent of how his parents would go above and beyond to meet a customer's need. Furthermore, he encouraged a spirit of innovation and a willingness to challenge the status quo, drawing inspiration from the Socratic method of questioning everything to find deeper truths and better solutions. This blend of values created a robust culture that drove the company forward.

Additionally, John was an active member of The Executive Committee, a well-recognized global leadership development organization for business leaders. "This group was a tremendous resource," he noted. "We met monthly to discuss leadership challenges and exchange strategies, which proved invaluable in navigating the complexities of managing a growing firm."

Reflecting on what he believed would make his developing company successful, John shared, "The true indicators of our success were our clients' successes and our ability to adapt to the constantly changing market environment."

Discussing the role of mistakes in the company's growth, John acknowledged their inevitability and value. "Of course, there have been stumbles along the way," he conceded. "You don't just learn from successes; mistakes are often where the most valuable lessons come from. It's about constantly moving forward, adapting, and evolving."

He noted that some funds were liquidated when demand for a particular product did not materialize as expected. Closing these products enabled the firm to reallocate resources more effectively, ensuring they were aligned with existing client needs and the overall strategic direction of the company.

To facilitate this continuous improvement, John held regular leadership meetings. "I believe in frequent one-on-ones," he noted, indicating his hands-on approach to management. "While we may not meet weekly, our meetings are frequent enough to ensure we are proactive rather than reactive."

He also discussed the importance of maintaining a strong company culture, especially as the business grew. He considered it vital that the firm not lose its identity even as it expanded, and the key to this was giving every employee the attention they needed to fit in with the company and their coworkers by aligning their goals with the group.

This nurturing approach, John explained, was about creating a supportive environment that mirrored a family setting, which he believed was crucial for maintaining morale and productivity in a high-pressure industry.

John's early adoption of technology not only set a precedent for his company but also significantly influenced his success trajectory. He was among the first to recognize the potential of emerging technologies in the financial sector. "I was one of the early adopters of Apple computers, learning to handle everything myself," John recounted, illustrating his hands-on approach to innovation.

This initiative was crucial during the early days, enabling him to leverage technology to constantly streamline operations and enhance analytical capabilities.

John eventually built a dedicated tech team whose impact was felt across the entire business. They created client management software, developed spreadsheet models for the research team and portfolio managers, and built proprietary in-house business intelligence tools for client communications, sales reporting, and financial modeling.

Using dashboards and technology to manage risk and reward in a complex, ever-changing environment was a natural step for this O-2 pilot. His team knew him for his relentless drive to improve systems and find better ways to manage the business. "It really is a constant initiative," John confirmed, underscoring the ongoing effort to maintain cutting-edge financial technology.

This strategic focus not only kept his company competitive but also demonstrated his foresight in integrating technology with traditional investment strategies.

Chapter 12

A Journey Home

Peter, John's father, embodied the hardworking ethos typical of Greek immigrants in America. His commitment to providing for his family was unwavering, and his life in the United States was characterized by the successful outcomes of their combined hard work.

Despite his deep roots in Greek heritage, Peter had not returned to Greece since he left in 1914. Nevertheless, his pride in his homeland seemingly never waned. When anyone expressed admiration for the beauty of a landscape or the vibrancy of flowers, Peter would nostalgically reply, "You should see it in Greece!"

Peter's expressed fondness for his homeland was a recurring theme. For instance, John recalled as he and his siblings swam in Lake Michigan, Peter would often remark, "The water is far superior in Greece." These comments, although charming, usually made the children roll their eyes and say, "Here we go again."

When John's mother, Mary, passed away in 1979, her loss left a profound void in their lives. In the wake of her passing, John, understanding the deep importance of heritage and memory, suggested a trip with his family back to Greece—their ancestral homeland.

This journey was about more than returning to the country of their forefathers and Peter's youth; it offered a chance to deeply and profoundly reconnect with their origins, merging the past with their present lives. For John, the trip was a revealing adventure, discovering the place where his father grew up and connecting with the heritage that had influenced them both.

At the venerable age of 88, Peter would finally return to the village of his childhood. However, this trip was more than just a return to a place; it was a poignant journey through memories of a life once lived, now shared with his son.

John recalled a touching moment when Peter said, "I have to go see the man who gave me the money to go to America." With a gentle smile, John reminded him, "Dad, that was a long time ago." This exchange was particularly meaningful to John, highlighting his father's enduring gratitude for those who helped him, despite the many years that had passed.

Another memorable moment from the trip occurred shortly after John, his father, and John's children landed in Athens. As they took a cab to their hotel, their driver pointed out some flowers and remarked, "Aren't those beautiful?" Without missing a beat, Peter responded, "You should see the flowers in America!"

John was astonished by his father's remark and recalled, "If I'd had a cell phone back then, I would have immediately called my siblings to say, 'you wouldn't believe what Dad just said!'" This light-hearted yet profound comment underscored Peter's deep affection for the country that had given him and his family a new beginning.

A major highlight of their journey was visiting Vourvoura, the quaint village where Peter spent his childhood. Nestled among lush olive groves and sprawling vineyards, it was everything Peter had described in his stories. This charming village, with its traditional stone houses and winding cobblestone streets, seemed untouched by time, offering a direct window into Peter's past and the rich cultural heritage of the region.

As father and son strolled through the village on unpaved roads, every corner and every view brought Peter's childhood to life, making the village feel both overwhelmingly familiar and enjoy-ably new to John. Eventually, the family arrived at the blue-and-white wooden house Peter had helped his father build decades ago. The enduring structure stood as a tangible link to Peter's past. As they approached, Peter's sister appeared on the porch, tears stream-ing down her face as she cried, "Pete!" She greeted them with the traditional Greek welcome dish—sour cherry preserves.

The well-preserved home, with its weathered stones and sturdy frame, symbolized the lasting impact of Peter's early life and efforts. It was a poignant reminder of his resilience and the enduring spirit he carried from those formative years into his life in America.

His father's stories came alive. "It just reminded him of so many things," John recalled.

The emotional impact of the experience was significant, not only from seeing the house but also from meeting distant relatives who, until then, had only been names in stories.

The trip was more than a return to their roots; it was a deep dive into the history that shaped both John and his father. While in Greece, they visited a local memorial honoring the villagers who stood against the Axis powers—mainly Italy and Germany—during World War II. This visit was unplanned and seeing the names of his own relatives among the fallen heroes etched into the memorial moved John profoundly, highlighting their courage and sacrifice.

John's visit to the memorial brought to mind Oxi Day, a significant day in Greek history commemorated on October 28 each year. This national holiday, also known as the *Day of No*, marks the moment in 1940 during World War II when Greek Prime Minister Ioannis Metaxas famously refused Italian dictator Benito Mussolini's demand to allow Axis forces to enter Greece. This defiance, which marked the first time a country had stood its ground in this way, inspired countries around the world to stand together in an alliance that would ultimately lead to Germany's defeat.

John also recalled the famous quote attributed to Winston Churchill that celebrated the indomitable spirit of the Greeks: "Until now we used to say that the Greeks fight like heroes. Now we shall say: Heroes fight like Greeks."

Peter, who had spent decades adapting to a new country, found himself seeing his old home through the eyes of both the boy he had been and the man he had become. And for John, it was a profound connection to his heritage, a thread that extended back through generations, now woven into his own identity.

In reflecting on the trip, John noted that the whole experience—from the sight of the house to encounters with relatives and time spent in the village—reinforced the significance of his Greek heritage and underscored the importance of remembering his roots.

Returning to Greece was a deeply emotional experience for Peter, rekindling memories of his youth and reconnecting with his roots. For John, the experience deepened his connection to his heritage, serving as a poignant reminder of his family's origins and their collective journey.

Chapter 13

Strategies for Stability

A s John built his firm in the late 1970s, his guiding philosophy was clear: constant innovation was essential to adapting to the rapid market changes of the time, marked by economic turbulence including oil crises, soaring inflation, and volatile interest rates. He recognized early on that navigating these challenges required not just reacting to market changes but also proactively preparing for them.

He also understood that sustained success depended on a client-centric approach, where anticipating shifts and developing tailored strategies were essential for thriving in an ever-changing financial landscape.

While serving in the Air Force in the late 1960s, John discovered convertible securities and developed a keen interest in them. John quickly recognized that their ability to manage market volatility would become a cornerstone of his investment strategy. "Convertible bonds gave us a way to stay in the game when the market was unpredictable," he recalls.

This insight complemented John's strong understanding of options, enabling him to integrate both into his strategies. He tailored each client's portfolio to their unique risk-reward profile, effectively managing risk while pursuing growth opportunities. "You can't wait until after a downturn to manage risk. It has to be built into your strategy from day one," John often emphasized, a philosophy that continues to guide the firm today.

In the early to mid-1980s, soaring interest rates, which peaked at about 20% to combat inflation, and a volatile stock market created a challenging environment for even seasoned investors. It felt like the financial world was shifting under everyone's feet, forcing investors to reconsider their strategies.

The Federal Reserve's aggressive rate hikes under Paul Volcker made borrowing expensive and led to poor stock market performance, causing widespread economic uncertainty.

During this period, investors sought more stable, risk-managed strategies to navigate the volatile market conditions. This environment provided an opportunity for innovative approaches, such as those involving convertible bonds and options. "We stayed focused on our roots and on managing risk," John explains. "By sticking with convertible bonds, we had a tool that balanced risk and reward, even in tough markets."

In 1983, John's nephew, Nick Calamos—son of his brother Angelo—joined the firm fresh out of college, eager to immerse himself in the investment world. Initially working as a computer programmer, Nick recognized the transformative power of technology and focused on integrating computerized research.

"Nick led the development of the firm's proprietary research system, bringing a new dimension to the firm by enhancing our analytical capabilities with cutting-edge technology," John recalled, acknowledging how his nephew built on the foundation he had established.

This marked the beginning of the firm's transformation, dedicated to meeting client needs through advanced technological tools in its investment strategies. Nick would ultimately emerge as a respected leader within the organization.

"Curiosity and a willingness to work hard toward a shared goal are tremendously valuable in hiring," John explained. "One common mistake business owners make is prioritizing years of experience above all else. Of course, for certain roles, experience is crucial," he acknowledged, "but individuals earlier in their careers can add a lot to a team. They bring diverse perspectives, fresh ideas, and strategies for leveraging newer technologies."

John believed this mindset allowed his firm to grow by embracing the potential of younger talent. It was about fostering a culture where fresh thinking could thrive, benefiting both the team and the business.

John continued, "Sometimes you see a spark in someone—a natural intellectual curiosity. Mentor them. Give them the runway and invest in them. Nick's success at Calamos and what we built together exemplifies that." He added, "He played an essential role in shaping the firm's direction and success, contributing to our ability to evolve and innovate."

Additionally, John's focus on the options market complemented his work with convertibles, as he integrated selling options against stocks to bolster his proactive, defensive approach. This strategy highlighted his ability to anticipate market trends and the importance of staying ahead. As John often remarked, "You don't want to get in the car with an economist because he's always looking in the rearview mirror."

This lighthearted comment reflected John's core philosophy: anticipating market changes rather than reacting to them. This proactive approach guided him and his clients successfully through decades of market fluctuations, laying the groundwork for industry recognition after the stock market crash of 1987.

Even in the wake of the crash, Calamos Investments stood out, earning its first of many Lipper Awards. These prestigious awards recognize funds and management firms that excel in delivering consistently strong, risk-adjusted performance.

Winning during such a turbulent period highlighted the firm's ability to safeguard and grow investor capital, setting a standard of excellence that would define its reputation for years to come.

In 1988, building on the success of his convertible fund, John expanded into international markets, targeting regions like Japan and Europe, both known for their issuance of convertible securities. "We saw opportunities globally that we couldn't ignore," John recalled. "Convertibles were gaining traction in Japan and Europe, and we wanted to be at the forefront of that market." This move marked a pivotal step into global diversification, demonstrating his foresight and commitment to keeping the firm at the cutting edge of the financial world.

This global expansion, coupled with his deep expertise in convertible securities, inspired John to write *Investing in Convertible Securities: Your Complete Guide to the Risks and Rewards*. Published in 1988, his book sought to demystify convertible bonds and provide a comprehensive guide for investors at all levels, eager to leverage the unique advantages of convertibles. "I wanted to break down the complexities and show that convertibles are a powerful tool for managing risk while participating in equity markets," John explained.

That same year, John expanded his investment strategy by launching a fund that sought both capital appreciation and income generation. The fund leveraged the firm's expertise in convertible securities, combining them with other investment types to create a winning formula.

By targeting a diversified portfolio of growth-oriented stocks and convertible securities, the fund was designed for investors seeking a lower-volatility approach to the stock market. "History has shown that stocks perform well over the long term, but they can be volatile in the short term. I wanted to combine convertibles and stocks to help investors manage that volatility.

"When you can provide a way to reduce some of the market's ups and downs, it encourages investors to stay invested for the long term and avoid selling during short-term downturns," John explained.

By 1990, John's firm had established itself as a leader in the asset management industry by launching one of the first liquid alternative mutual funds. This initiative demonstrated his commitment to giving individual investors access to sophisticated strategies typically reserved for institutions.

The fund used a market-neutral strategy to provide income and consistent performance regardless of market direction, without taking on much interest rate opportunity or risk. By doing so, the fund sought to provide bond-like income, without the volatility of bonds.

Unlike traditional bond portfolios, John's strategy created a lower-risk, more steady investment that reduced exposure to interest rate risks through convertible arbitrage, which capitalizes on price inefficiencies between convertible securities and their underlying stocks.

"Convertible arbitrage was a natural extension of our expertise. We offered investors a way to exploit market inefficiencies without sacrificing stability, managing interest rate risks more effectively than a traditional fixed-income strategy," John explained, highlighting the innovative edge of the approach.

At the time, the concept was relatively new and not widely understood, requiring John and his team to educate the financial community. Alternative strategies were typically the domain of large institutional investors, and the potential of these sophisticated tools was unfamiliar to many financial advisors and individual investors.

Even data providers struggled to categorize them. John and his team had to both promote the market-neutral fund and explain the benefits of using convertible securities and alternative strategies to enhance returns and manage risk.

This commitment to financial literacy underscored his mission to develop sophisticated financial products accessible to a broader range of investors. John expanded the sales team to include individuals with advanced and specialized training, such as Certified Public Accountants and Chartered Financial Analysts.

He also provided training on how to position sophisticated investments in client portfolios. The trading desk, research team, and portfolio management teams grew and developed highly interactive ways to coordinate their efforts.

Reflecting on the challenge of educating potential clients and partners, John shared, "The biggest hurdle was explaining it clearly enough for people to grasp the strategy and see its benefits."

One particularly memorable incident occurred when the fund rating agency Morningstar mistakenly categorized Calamos's market-neutral fund as an equity fund. "When we launched it, and the market corrected, our fund performed well, which led everyone to think, 'What a great equity fund!' They didn't realize we were actually using a different strategy altogether," John clarified.

Looking back on the early days of promoting these funds, John emphasized his hands-on approach: "I was deeply involved. One of the advantages of flying my own plane was that it allowed me to travel across the country for presentations. I met with major brokerage firms like Merrill Lynch and Morgan Stanley, individual clients, and visited the companies we were investing in. Members of my team came with me, and we educated clients together."

This commitment to direct engagement not only enabled John to build strong relationships with key stakeholders but also to convey the unique value proposition of his approach in a compelling way. "It was essential for me to show that I was not just asking for their business but truly believing in the potential of what we were offering," he emphasized. By personally connecting with potential investors and partners, he ensured that his vision and innovative strategies were clearly communicated, fostering trust and confidence in his approach.

As his firm expanded, John recognized the need to continue growing his team. "I couldn't handle everything alone," he admitted, emphasizing the importance of training his team to master and implement the complex strategies that set Calamos Investments apart from others in the industry.

"Throughout the '90s, we capitalized on growth sectors like the burgeoning internet, which was much like AI is today," John noted. His firm established a growth fund specifically targeting these emerging sectors, achieving remarkable success throughout the decade.

By the late 1990s, as the market surged, John's strategic foresight prompted him to hedge their investments against emerging risks. "We started noticing signs of overvaluation in equities as the decade came to a close," John recalled. In response, his team took precautionary steps, including buying put options to safeguard their positions.

This prudent approach, reflective of the firm's careful management, enabled them to navigate a period of significant growth and volatility. Although the strategy initially appeared less effective, it proved invaluable when the market eventually corrected. "It really helped us a lot," John reflected, recognizing the importance of their cautious planning during turbulent times.

"Managing risk is far more important than trying to time the market," he asserted, a philosophy that became foundational to his strategy. He focused on steady, disciplined risk management, prioritizing long-term success over fleeting gains. Ultimately, John's mission was not focused on the excitement of outperforming the market but on protecting and growing his clients' investments and building a resilient company that could weather any storm.

This thoughtful and patient approach to risk management and growth laid the foundation for his future endeavors, serving as a blueprint for how he would develop his firm.

It created a framework that ensured lasting success for both the business and the clients it served.

Chapter 14

A Journey Together

"You can't be successful if you go it alone," John often says. For him, teamwork is what carried him through life-or-death moments in the skies over Vietnam. That same principle of teamwork became the cornerstone of Calamos Investments, helping it evolve from a small business with a few clients into a global investment manager known for its expertise in risk-managed investment strategies.

Among all the teams in John's life, one holds a special place in his heart: his marriage to Mae Calamos. Built on shared values, deep respect, and enduring love, their partnership touches every part of his life—family, business, and philanthropy.

"I couldn't ask for a better person to be by my side. I've got a lot of irons in the fire, and I'm truly grateful for her unwavering support. I couldn't have done any of this without her," John reflects.

John and Mae's meeting was purely a matter of chance. By this time, John's first marriage had ended in divorce, and as Calamos Investments grew, the demands of building the business became nearly all-consuming. However, John still found ways to recharge. Flying remained his favorite way to do so, but he also found new outlets in golf and tennis.

In 1992, one morning at his tennis club, John overheard a conversation that caught his attention. Mae Witkowski, chatting with a doctor, mentioned her interest in a receptionist position the doctor was looking to fill. Having previously played tennis with Mae, John was impressed by her warm and professional demeanor and thought she would be a perfect fit for his front office.

So before he left, he stopped to ask if she was really looking for a new job. Surprised yet intrigued, Mae responded, "Yes, I am." John promptly handed her his business card and said, "I think I have an opportunity for you."

Mae joined the team at John's Oak Brook office, initially coming on board to manage the front desk, where she quickly became known for her excellent interpersonal skills. John noticed how effectively Mae connected with both staff and clients, her ease reflecting years of experience handling challenging situations when she had been a flight attendant.

One day, shortly after Mae joined the firm, John noticed she seemed quieter than he knew her to be. He approached her desk to ask about her impressions of the office environment.

"So, what do you think of Calamos?" he asked. Mae responded nervously, "Do you want my honest opinion?" When John assured her he did, she said, "Well, you know what? It's like working in a morgue."

John laughed in surprise and asked for more details. Mae explained, "You walk in, and everyone is so quiet—that's just not me." John replied, "Well, just be yourself, Mae." This advice proved to be a turning point for her.

"Mae always looks for ways to make things better, and she has a real gift for creating warmth and energy," said John. Mae's influence, combined with John's encouragement of her true personality, reshaped the office culture, proving that one person's authenticity can transform an entire workplace. The office became a lively and welcoming environment.

In their interactions, Mae observed John was a soft-spoken leader, yet his passion and strength subtly commanded respect and set a definitive tone throughout the workplace. "He's a very quiet, shy man; he's strong, he's passionate with what he does, and that's what he radiates," Mae explained, highlighting John's subtle but impactful leadership style.

Mae's career at Calamos Investments and her personal relationship with John both flourished over time. As they worked together, their mutual respect for one another grew, and they realized they had a great deal in common beyond tennis, finding shared values in hard work, dedication to excellence, and a strong commitment to family.

Over the years, what began as a professional partnership evolved surprisingly into a deep, personal bond, culminating in marriage. "If someone had told me we'd end up where we are today, I wouldn't have believed it," Mae admitted, reflecting on how they both valued their independence but naturally grew closer over time.

Their eventual decision to marry was spontaneous and nontraditional, epitomized by a quick getaway to Las Vegas. They chose a simple ceremony without much prior planning, deciding impulsively one weekend to tie the knot in a small chapel they found online.

"What are we doing this weekend? Hey, let's go to Vegas," John suggested, leading to an impromptu wedding attended only by John's brother, Angelo, and his wife, who were told of the wedding only once they were aboard John's plane.

Despite the initial exclusivity of their Vegas wedding, the family celebrated their union later with a larger party, and in 2015, the couple would renew their vows in a traditional ceremony at a Greek church, involving their entire family and making it a significant and inclusive celebration. "We had a big, beautiful Greek wedding, everyone was part of it," Mae said, recalling the joy she and John felt at having everyone together.

As the business grew, John increasingly relied on Mae's skills, particularly when he moved the company to its new headquarters on Warrenville Road in Naperville, Illinois. Calamos occupied most of the building, but John leased portions of the building to other businesses.

Following the sudden departure of a tenant, John faced a decision about how to use the half-floor that had been vacated. John, consistently impressed by Mae's ability to transform workplace atmospheres since her first days at Calamos, asked her to manage the setup for short-term rentals.

With her characteristic entrepreneurial zeal, Mae embraced the challenge, repurposing the vacant space effectively. She developed preliminary plans and collaborated with an architect to refine her ideas.

"I did all the research and then presented John with the idea," Mae explained. John liked every bit of what he saw, and simply responded, "Hey, go for it."

With John's enthusiastic support, Mae launched the Primacy Business Center, establishing it as a premier venue, offering flexible office solutions akin to modern coworking spaces, in the Chicago suburbs. "She created this," John explained proudly, highlighting Mae's pivotal role in transforming a vacant space into a thriving business center that significantly boosted the company's portfolio and reputation.

The success of Primacy, initiated by John and Mae's collaborative efforts, set a precedent that was later mirrored in the development of a larger headquarters as Calamos Investments expanded. This growth not only reflected their enduring partnership but also had a lasting impact on the community and the firm.

The new Calamos Campus embodied this spirit, blending corporate functionality with hospitality, creating a welcoming environment for both employees and visitors. This expansion was a testament to how their shared vision had become a cornerstone of the company's identity and growth strategy.

John's vision for the new headquarters at 2020 Calamos Court in Naperville was deeply influenced by his passion for design and architecture and aimed to create more than just a functional workspace. Inspired by Mae's ability to create warm and inviting spaces, John envisioned an office that would not only meet practical needs but also inspire pride and reflect the company's success, while embodying the spirit of hospitality and community that she valued.

Initially, the plan was simply to build a new, larger office building, but as more property became available, John's vision expanded. He strategically purchased additional land not only to prevent unwanted developments but also with future office expansion in mind.

The sleek, multistory structure, made of glass and steel, paid tribute to John's architectural hero, Mies van der Rohe. It was also one of the first privately developed buildings in the area to be registered under the LEED® (Leadership in Energy and Environmental Design) Green Building Rating System.

To bring this vision to life, John collaborated with Mies van der Rohe's grandson, architect Dirk Lohan, ensuring the design reflected the iconic style of his grandfather. Both Lohan and John share an alma mater, having graduated from Illinois Tech, which deepened their connection and mutual understanding throughout the design and construction process.

This collaboration resulted in a building that not only pays tribute to Mies van der Rohe's legacy but also stands as a testament to John's commitment to excellence in architecture. The top two floors of the building emphasize open space, reflecting the surrounding prairie. A kinetic spiral staircase connects the upper floor, which includes John's corner office and library, to an open ceiling that overlooks the busy trading desk below. Every day, John is surrounded by the activity of the markets.

The décor of the new campus also blends both Mae's Native American heritage and John's Greek roots, enriching the cultural richness of the environment.

Mae's role grew to encompass managing not only office space but also new expansions that were added to the company's real estate portfolio. John found her oversight crucial in easing his workload, enabling him to focus more on the investment side of the business. "She was extremely helpful," he noted, appreciating how her management significantly reduced the operational challenges associated with their real estate and hospitality ventures.

Similar to his approach with investment tools, the development of John's business campus evolved organically, not from a grand initial plan but in response to emerging needs and opportunities.

Observing the lack of superior lodging accommodation options in the area, John envisioned a hotel facility that would serve guests but also enrich the local infrastructure. "With our global visitors in mind, I thought we should build a world-class hotel," John explained, highlighting the strategic decision to provide top-tier accommodations for international clients. "But Mae was the one who brought it to life."

Completed in 2008, the hotel stands as a testament to John and Mae's partnership and shared vision, blending luxury with unique cultural elements. Named Hotel Arista (where *Arista* means "the best" in Greek), it is the tallest building in Naperville and represents the pinnacle of accommodation and service.

Featuring a sleek steel and glass design like the Calamos headquarters just across the campus, the hotel serves as a striking centerpiece of CityGate Centre and includes a spa, fitness center, restaurants, a ballroom, and bars, catering to international visitors and significantly boosting the local economy.

The construction of the hotel marked the beginning of John and Mae's deeper involvement in real estate. "We also worked together to expand CityGate Centre by constructing another office building and apartment complex, which marked our formal entry into the real estate sector," John explained.

The initial project naturally developed into a comprehensive corporate campus, complete with facilities that supported core business operations as well as the general public. "There's no way I could have done this without Mae. Her ability to connect with people and her dedication were crucial as the business diversified into real estate and hospitality. She's transformed CityGate Centre into a space that's both welcoming and vibrant, engaging directly with employees and guests to create a community-like atmosphere."

Mae often joins staff for lunch, offers help in the kitchen, or makes her rounds through the buildings, ensuring everyone feels appreciated. "Thank you for being here. We can't do this without you," is a frequent expression of her gratitude, emphasizing the value she sees in every team member.

Her involvement extends deeply into operations as well. As chief operating officer for Calamos Property Holdings, which includes both real estate and hospitality, she meets with her teams regularly to ensure her high standards are upheld across the businesses. She actively supports all levels of the operation, ensuring that clients and guests receive the highest level of service, even in the smallest details.

"If someone isn't satisfied with their food or service, I'll make sure to take care of it right away," she asserts, highlighting her hands-on approach to management and her commitment to excellence. This personal touch extends throughout the establishment, making guests feel as though they are being welcomed into her home, not just a business.

With Mae by his side, John has had a steadfast partner through the toughest times. "In some ways, we couldn't have chosen a worse time to launch CityGate," he reflected. "It was right before the global financial crisis hit in 2008, but we just stayed focused on our goals and the long-term. Neither of us are quitters."

And the shared perseverance paid off. Despite the timing and the ensuing economic downturn, the hotel project was a rewarding venture. "The hotel was so much fun to be involved in," Mae reminisced, reflecting on the excitement and creativity involved in creating a high-standard facility.

She reflects on her journey from being a flight attendant to playing a significant role in the development and management of a major business center, a transition that amazes even her. "You can do whatever you want in life, in America. How badly do you want something?" she muses, emphasizing the power of determination and effort—a trait she shares with John.

Navigating the dual roles of business partners and spouses brings its own set of challenges, but Mae and John find a balance that works for them. Their relationship thrives on mutual respect and autonomy within their professional domains. "He lets me do my thing, and I let him do his," Mae shares, highlighting the trust and independence that characterize their working relationship.

This respect extends to problem-solving in the business, with John supporting Mae's decisions on operational issues like staffing and customer service.

Family life remains largely distinct from business discussions. When they are with family, especially their children and grandchildren, the focus shifts entirely to personal matters. "When our children and grandchildren come, it's all about family," Mae emphasized, noting that business talk is minimal during these times.

However, she acknowledges that complete separation isn't always possible. "I'm not going to say there's no talk of business, but it's little things," she explains, reflecting the natural overlap given their intertwined professional and personal lives.

This story highlights the enduring growth and deepening of Mae and John's relationship, demonstrating how they successfully balance their independence with their partnership. Together, they seamlessly integrate their lives while maintaining a profound respect for each other's autonomy.

Their relationship is further strengthened by their shared values, which fortify their bond and enrich their journey together. This harmonious blend not only enhances their mutual experience but also epitomizes a relationship built on love, respect, and shared growth.

Chapter 15

A Lifelong Passion for Flight

John's passion for flying, sparked in his youth, became a defining aspect of his life during his Air Force career. Commissioned as an officer on his graduation from Illinois Tech in 1963, he was eager to serve his country as the Vietnam War escalated. Military pilot training in Texas was both intense and transformative, pushing John to sharpen his focus and master the demands of high-performance aviation.

Through rigorous training, he developed the skills needed to fly supersonic jets like the T-38 Talon, which became his favorite aircraft. "The speed and agility were incredible," he reflected. Completing the program, he earned his wings—a proud moment that marked his transition from a novice to a highly skilled aviator. This foundation would prepare him for the challenges he would later face in Vietnam.

Reflecting on his time as a forward air controller, John shared, "Oh, yeah, I had a lot of close calls." It was in the heat of those moments that he truly grasped the value of his training, mentorship, and the ability to stay calm under pressure. In the brutal and unforgiving nature of warfare, where split-second decisions meant the difference between life and death, those lessons proved indispensable.

John's training instilled in him a methodical approach to flying, emphasizing the importance of staying focused and composed. His ability to maintain calm during crises allowed him to instinctively think, "Okay, let's take this step; let's do this."

Each challenge he encountered in the sky transformed him into a resilient leader. His calmness and determination under pressure became hallmarks of both his flying style and his business approach.

A critical component of John's training was the use of check-lists. "Okay, this is happening. What do we do? What's next?" he explained, highlighting how these procedures ensured that every step was meticulously followed. His training as an instrument-rated pilot equipped him to handle various flying conditions, including low visibility.

In California, John and his crew practiced flying the B-52 at low altitudes, often with the cockpit shades closed to rely solely on instruments. "One pilot could look out the window to avoid crashing, while the other flew based on instruments," he noted, recognizing how essential this training was, especially in the event of a nuclear detonation where visibility could be severely compromised.

Flying the massive B-52 close to the ground, particularly in the mountainous terrain of Nevada and California, posed unique challenges. "It was unnerving, but it was part of the job," John admitted. These intense practice missions sharpened his skills and deepened his understanding of aviation's complexities, reinforcing the vital lessons he would carry throughout his career.

John's passion for aviation extended to a variety of aircraft, each serving distinct purposes throughout his flying career. One of his first airplanes was a Grumman Tiger, which he purchased with an Air Force friend. This aircraft allowed him to fly from Chicago to Grissom Air Force Base for his time in the Reserves, significantly reducing travel time compared to the three-hour drive. "That was my first little airplane that I flew," John recalled.

After a few years with the Grumman Tiger, John upgraded to the MU-2F, an aircraft recommended by another Air Force buddy. The MU-2F, known for its speed and versatility, is a twin-engine turboprop that can cruise at speeds up to 300 knots and has a range of about 1,800 nautical miles. With a spacious cabin for six to eight passengers and advanced avionics, it became a favorite for both business and personal travel.

As his business expanded, John transitioned to the Learjet 25D and then the Beechjet 400, which allowed for even more passengers. "The MU-2F was a propeller-driven plane, so moving to the Beechjet with jet engines was just an upgrade for me," he explained. The Beechjet's speed and efficiency made it an ideal choice for his growing travel needs.

Through his diverse experiences with various aircraft, John developed a deep understanding of aviation, risk management, and the importance of adaptability, both in flying and in business. Preparation and methodical thinking were key to his flying experience. John kept his pilot's license current and completed pilot "check out" evaluations for all the planes he owned to ensure his skills remained sharp.

His mindset became vitally important during a tense moment behind the control of his Beechjet. While flying at nearly 40,000 feet, John served as the pilot in command, with Mae seated in the back alongside a friend.

Suddenly, the air cycle machine—responsible for providing cool air for pressurization—suffered a critical failure when the pressure switch malfunctioned, causing the system to shut down. Without the normal airflow for pressurization, John asked the copilot to manually select emergency mode, as high-temperature air and smoke began to flood the cabin.

John and his copilot quickly assessed the dire situation. The cabin filled with a deafening roar as the emergency system kicked in.

Inside, the temperature soared as the air, no longer cooled by the air cycle machine, entered the cabin at a staggering 700° F. The heat was so intense that the adhesive on the headliner began to melt, causing the leather to droop.

The gravity of the situation set in immediately. Without cabin pressure, the time to useful consciousness was critically short, and John was acutely aware of the risks. Everyone aboard donned oxygen masks as John and his copilot dove the aircraft down, troubleshooting the issue while maintaining control.

In the back, Mae felt the oppressive heat, and as a former flight attendant, knew that something was seriously wrong. When she looked up, she saw John's calm expression focused on the emergency procedures. He was carefully preparing the aircraft for descent, which reassured her amid the chaos.

As the situation escalated, John maintained the rapid descent to a breathable altitude. "It was hot, and the drop was fast, like the bottom had just fallen out," John recalled. Despite the discomfort and sudden loss of altitude, John's steady control kept everyone calm.

While descending to a safer altitude, he and his copilot diligently worked through the checklist, assessing the situation. Initially alarmed by the air from the engines, they knew they wouldn't go above 15,000 feet until landing safely. Reaching breathable altitudes, they switched off the emergency pressurization mode, flying at 11,000 feet now comfortably unpressurized as they diverted to Pueblo, Colorado.

Ultimately, they discovered that the cabin pressure issues came from a failure of the pressure switch in the air cycle machine, not the pressurization system itself, according to copilot Joe Dougherty. This machine is crucial for keeping the cabin comfortable; it takes hot "bleed" air from the engines and turns it into cooler, conditioned air. Plus, it helps maintain cabin pressurization, which is important for the safety and comfort of everyone on board at high altitudes.

In another memorable incident, Dougherty became momentarily distracted during a high-workload moment while taxiing in the Beechjet. During a crucial boost pump check, which ensures the fuel system's pumps are functioning properly, the pumps were inadvertently left off.

As they climbed, Joe noticed a slight fuel imbalance and suggested cross-feeding the fuel. John agreed, but as soon as the cross-feed was selected, a red master warning light illuminated, followed by low fuel pressure warnings for both the left and right tanks. "My heart was racing," Joe recalled. "Red lights are never a good sign in an airplane."

Realizing his mistake, Joe instinctively reached up to the overhead panel to switch the boost pumps back on. But John, ever the composed pilot, swiftly raised his hand to block Joe's move. "Hold on," John cautioned. "The engines are running. Let's take stock of the situation and see what's happening here."

Joe remembers how John's calm demeanor grounded him in the moment. "John had this way of slowing things down when everything felt chaotic," Joe said. "He reminded me to understand the situation first, before rushing into action."

Once they had assessed the situation and were on the same page, Joe suggested turning the pumps back on. "I asked John if we should turn them back on, and he gave the nod," Joe recalled. As soon as they activated the boost pumps, the warning lights extinguished, and the situation stabilized.

It was in those moments of crisis that John entered a focused state, assessing and prioritizing the steps needed to rectify the issue. The lessons he learned in the cockpit extended far beyond flying.

One notable plane in John's collection is the Marchetti SF 260. He was immediately drawn to its impressive performance, describing it as a propeller-driven aircraft that flew almost like a jet. This aircraft became a favorite among his friends and fellow reservists, particularly Wendell Green, who enjoyed flying it whenever he could.

"This airplane is really special," John recalled fondly. "It felt like a military aircraft." The Marchetti, known for its agility and speed, earned the nickname *la Ferrari del Cielo*, or the Ferrari of the Sky. As a tribute to his time in the service—and because the US Air Force had evaluated John's particular model as a potential primary pilot training aircraft—he had it painted in military camouflage.

Initially, he used the aircraft for both business and pleasure. "When I first got it, if I was going to a client meeting in Colorado, I would jump in the airplane, have my meetings, and then fly back home," he said. This flexibility enabled him to blend work with his passion for flying.

"I still have it; it's in my hangar," he added proudly.

John's journey as a pilot not only honed his technical skills but also molded him into a resilient leader. Each challenge faced in the air contributed to his growth, enabling him to navigate the complexities of both flying and running a successful business. His experiences reinforced the belief that teamwork, preparation, and focus are fundamental to overcoming obstacles and achieving shared goals.

As John's business expanded internationally, so too did the demand for overseas travel. With the need for more efficient long-haul flights, he transitioned from the Cessna CE-750 Citation X to the Falcon 7X, which revolutionized his travel capabilities.

John valued the advanced technology in the 7X, which made flying smoother, though it came with a bit of a learning curve. Although he flew the plane when he first bought it, he quickly realized how intricate it was. "It was pretty sophisticated, with a lot of high-tech systems," he said. So, he decided to leave the flying to his skilled and experienced pilots.

The Falcon 7X enabled him to fly nonstop from Chicago to any destination in Europe, eliminating the need for fuel stops in the north. This efficiency was a game changer, particularly for business engagements that required promptness.

The Falcon 7X turned out to be an incredibly versatile aircraft, giving John the ability to travel internationally with ease. As soon as he got the plane, they tested its range and efficiency. "We flew the 7X from our hangar in West Chicago to Sapporo, Japan, nonstop," John recalled, impressed by what the aircraft could do. Just two months later, he was back on it for a business trip to South Korea.

With seating for about 15 passengers and 3–4 crew members, the 7X quickly became a key asset. It was not only fast and efficient but also offered a comfortable flying experience, frequently cruising at altitudes of 45,000 feet. Its speed, fuel efficiency, and spacious design made long-distance travel feel effortless, enabling John to manage global business engagements with ease.

"Joe Dougherty and Dave Laub are my captains on it. They have been with me for more than 20 years and have become family," John noted, emphasizing the importance of having experienced and trusted professionals at the controls.

Reflecting on his extensive flying experience, John drew parallels between aviation and the financial markets. He recognized that the principles of risk management were essential in both arenas. "Looking ahead and getting the right information is crucial," he explained. Each flight and every aircraft represented a chapter in his journey, showcasing not only his love for flying but also the invaluable lessons learned along the way.

After decades of soaring through the skies, John faced the difficult decision to step away from the pilot seat, realizing that his eyesight was becoming impaired and could affect his flying capabilities. It was a bittersweet moment; the cockpit had always been a sanctuary where he felt most alive.

"I stopped flying so I wouldn't put myself or my passengers at risk," he reflected, accepting the loss of something that had been such a defining part of his life. Letting go wasn't easy, but John understood that being a responsible pilot meant always putting safety first.

The same mindset guided him in business—managing risk and making thoughtful decisions were key to long-term success. Though he might not be at the controls, flying would always remain a part of his life, shaping his perspective and fueling his passion for new horizons.

A Lifelong Passion for Flight

Chapter 16

Calamos Goes Public

In the late 1990s and early 2000s, the tech boom dramatically transformed the world of finance, deeply integrating technology into every aspect of economic transactions and business operations.

Jim Pavalon, vice president of IT Systems Support and Computer Operations at Calamos Investments, emphasized, "John has always prioritized cutting-edge technology at the firm. He understands its critical role in our operations."

He noted how John's proactive approach included fostering strong connections with Illinois Tech where he served on the board. "These connections have facilitated valuable introductions and partnerships, keeping us at the forefront of technological advancements," Jim added.

During this period, the mutual fund industry experienced substantial growth, driven by increased market access and a surge in retail investors seeking diversified investment opportunities. This environment enabled firms like Calamos Investments to expand their reach significantly.

The convergence of technology and financial services also played a crucial role, streamlining processes and enhancing the capabilities of mutual fund managers. John's proactive approach to innovation kept Calamos at the forefront of these advancements, enabling the firm to adapt to changing market dynamics effectively.

As Calamos Investments grew, the increasing need for capital to support its expansion prompted John to consider taking the company public. He believed that going public would provide the necessary resources to enhance the firm's offerings, better meet client demands, and allow for reinvestment in operations. Transitioning from a private company to a public one would mark a significant change, but it was seen as a promising opportunity to open new doors for the firm.

"After much deliberation and discussions with trusted colleagues and my family's advisory I began to view going public as a significant advantage. It would allow us to secure the necessary capital to sustain our growth," John explained.

He viewed the transition to a public company not as a disruption but as a strategic opportunity. He was particularly optimistic about the potential to form a board of directors that could offer strategic guidance and help expand the business.

John envisioned a board with diverse expertise in finance, corporate governance, and strategic growth. He sought members capable of providing innovative insights and robust decision-making, aligned with Calamos Investments' goals for expansion and resilience.

Always focused on the company's well-being, John—inspired by Socrates—aimed for directors who were ready to challenge assumptions and ask critical questions, rather than merely rubber-stamping decisions. Assembling the board was straightforward, reflecting John's strong reputation and influence. "A good board brings a breadth of experience and a depth of knowledge that can challenge and refine our strategy, keeping us competitive and proactive," John explained.

He emphasized the need for board members who not only grasped the financial landscape but could also anticipate market trends and navigate the company through potential challenges. Recognizing the crucial role of these board members, he understood that their insight would be vital for the strategic planning and successful execution of the company's initial public offering (IPO).

John carefully considered the scope of the public offering, reflecting on the subjective nature of such strategic decisions. "It wasn't just about numbers; it was about what felt right for the company's future," he mused, emphasizing the thoughtful consideration behind taking Calamos Investments public.

He arranged the ownership and voting structure to retain control over the company. This approach enabled John and the Calamos family to maintain a majority of the voting power.

This setup was critical for John to continue guiding the company according to his vision. "Keeping control was really important to me. I wanted to make sure we could steer our future without too much interference from outside," John explained.

The decision to go public was a critical pivot in the company's history, mirroring the broader trends of the financial industry during that era, where integration of new market strategies and capital inflows were essential for sustained growth and innovation.

This industry-wide shift influenced John's strategic planning, underscoring the necessity of maintaining control during the IPO to adapt effectively and leverage these trends for the company's benefit.

As John got further into the IPO process, road shows became key. He and his team used these events to meet with institutional investors, analysts, and fund managers, highlighting the company's financial strengths and growth potential.

John excelled during the high-pressure road shows to persuade potential investors. His approach mirrored his interactions with his individual clients, using his enthusiasm to clearly communicate the company's value. "Talking about our plans and viewpoints with potential investors felt like familiar ground to me," he explained, underscoring his effectiveness in attracting investor support.

John's passion for aviation provided a practical advantage during the road shows. Owning his private jet streamlined travel logistics, ensuring timely arrivals for the demanding meeting schedule.

Although the nature of road shows has evolved with advancements in communication technology, in those days, they demanded

Calamos Goes Public

exhaustive in-person meetings. Despite this, John maintained a positive outlook on the process. "I enjoyed getting out there, meeting people, and explaining what we are all about," he recounted.

On October 27, 2004, the effective date of its IPO, Calamos Asset Management made a triumphant debut, raising $414 million, and the stock, initially priced at $18 on NASDAQ, ascended to the $25 range within weeks. By the close of 2006, Calamos Asset Management had a market capitalization of approximately $2.7 billion.

As planned, Calamos allocated the proceeds toward launching new strategies, enlarging staff and research capabilities, and financing the construction of a state-of-the-art headquarters in Naperville, designed by renowned architect Dirk Lohan.

As the business grew substantially, it wasn't just the firm's success that caught everyone's attention—John, the driving force behind it all, also became more prominent. Already familiar with media attention, John now found himself inundated with requests for his opinions and insights.

During this busy period, he received many accolades, but one stood out: the prestigious Ernst & Young Entrepreneur of the Year® award for the financial services sector in the Lake Michigan Area program in 2006. John was particularly humbled by this honor, as it marked a significant milestone in his entrepreneurial journey that had started many years earlier with his laundromats.

John's decision to take Calamos Investments public was a game changer for the company. It altered not just its structure but also how it operated and its culture. This shift initially caused some complications, especially in the way the company now had to communicate with its new board and shareholders.

Unlike the personal touch used in client interactions, which were closely tied to asset management, talking to shareholders required a more strategic approach. It was all about looking ahead, focusing on predictions and growth projections. This was a new kind of challenge for John, who was used to hands-on client management.

As John explained, "It was different. With shareholders, it's not just about the here and now. They are looking toward future growth, always anticipating the next big move. It's a bit more challenging to align everyone's expectations with the company's realistic goals.

"It wasn't just about managing funds; it was about managing perceptions, expectations, and maintaining trust in a much more public arena," John recalled.

During this era of public scrutiny and financial challenges, John and his team were compelled to reassess and adapt their strategies to thrive in their new public landscape. This shift highlighted the critical need for resilience and adaptability—traits that were not only crucial during the IPO process but became increasingly vital as the firm navigated the growing challenges leading up to the 2008 economic crisis.

This period served as a stark reminder that the strengths developed while overcoming the hurdles of going public would soon face even tougher tests, marking another defining chapter in the company's history.

Chapter 17

Weathering the Storm

In early 2007, the financial markets were already feeling the impact of troubling shifts that had begun the previous year. One of the most notable indicators was the steep decline in the US housing market, which had been a driving force of economic growth.

Housing prices, which had soared due to speculative investments and an abundance of easy credit, began to plummet in 2006, significantly reducing homeowners' equity and leading to an increase in mortgage defaults.

The stock market also showed signs of distress. Declines intensified as major financial institutions faced extreme pressure, culminating in the collapse of Lehman Brothers in September 2008. This was followed by a US government bailout of the global insurance company AIG.

Additionally, credit markets were seizing up. The spread between what banks charge each other for overnight loans and the Federal Reserve's benchmark rate widened dramatically, indicating a significant distrust in the banking sector.

Banks, wary of the financial stability of their counterparts, began to hoard cash, precipitating a lending freeze that affected businesses and consumers alike. This reluctance to lend led to a domino effect that exacerbated the already looming crisis, setting the stage for a financial meltdown that John observed with growing concern. "We witnessed the warning signs, but the sheer velocity and widespread impact of the crisis were staggering," he reflected.

As the crisis unfolded, catching Wall Street and the broader financial world off guard, Calamos Investments faced its own set of severe challenges. Like many others, the firm was roiled by the economic downturn.

"We, alongside so many others, hadn't anticipated a crisis of this scale, but we were forced to respond immediately," John explained, emphasizing the urgency with which they had to pivot their strategies to navigate the tumultuous financial waters.

Calamos Investments took strategic steps to recalibrate its product lines and investment strategies. Co-chief investment officer John Hillenbrand explained, "Our portfolio strategy always included a continuous evaluation of potential scenarios—base case, upside, and downside. This approach was incredibly valuable, especially in a rapidly changing environment. It gave our portfolio managers a strong framework to not only identify emerging risks but also to capitalize on eventual opportunities." This strategic foresight, rooted in John Calamos's foundational principles, enabled the firm not only to withstand the crisis but also to demonstrate the strength of its risk management and adaptability under pressure.

John, a staunch advocate for active management over passive index strategies, saw openings amid the changing market conditions. "We identified ways to translate short-term volatility into long-term opportunity. For example, convertible bonds typically offer lower yields in exchange for the option to convert the bond into stock. However, in many cases convertible bonds were now trading with yields similar to those of high yield bonds," John explained, illustrating the firm's ability to respond coolly and strategically in a crisis environment where many competitors acted rashly.

Adhering to his core investment philosophies, John and his team focused not only on mitigating near-term risks but also on maintaining a long-term perspective. John's investment team, including portfolio management and research, was guided by his beliefs that "the flipside of volatility is opportunity" and "there's opportunity in all markets." "We were constantly trying to provide a balance between the upside potential and downside risk," Hillenbrand explained, highlighting the firm's proactive approach.

As the crisis intensified, Calamos Investments faced significant challenges with their closed-end funds, particularly regarding Auction Rate Preferred Securities (ARPS). These securities, designed to be liquid through regular repricing and third-party liquidity events, suddenly lost their liquidity when these third parties withdrew.

"During parts of 2008, third parties decided not to provide any liquidity, leaving individual investors unable to sell their ARPS," Hillenbrand explained.

Despite the legalities allowing for such scenarios, John Calamos believed this was unjust for the shareholders. "Although the contract said that this could happen, and that was the risk they were taking on, we didn't think it was an appropriate way to treat our shareholders," John said.

Motivated by a duty to their clients and a desire to manage their funds with integrity, John spearheaded efforts to refinance these securities for those who wanted to exit them. The refinancing process was arduous, requiring the firm to find new lenders willing to provide the necessary funds during a time when the credit markets were nearly frozen.

"It was not the easiest thing to do during that time. But we were one of the first to undertake it, and John thought it was important," Hillenbrand noted. They eventually secured several short-term transactions to provide the needed liquidity.

This episode not only tested Calamos Investments' resolve but also reinforced their commitment to ethical financial management and client service. It exemplified John's philosophy, rooted in lessons from his parents' service in the family grocery store, of treating

111

investors with the utmost respect, responsiveness, and fairness. This approach further cemented his legacy as a leader who prioritized the well-being of his clients above all during one of the most challenging periods in financial history.

As turmoil cascaded through the global financial markets, a strategic decision to strengthen the firm's portfolio proved pivotal. In addition to taking measures designed to protect the value of the firm's corporate investment portfolio, Calamos moved to shore up its balance sheet. These actions placed Calamos Investments in a stronger position, but the company still faced significant challenges.

For asset managers such as Calamos, revenues are closely linked to assets under management. As asset values declined across markets a panicked selling and fear took hold, revenues also declined.

This period brought significant challenges across the organization, including for the sales team where Brian Waeyaert was a key senior member. "It was extremely stressful, to say the least," Waeyaert recalled. The crisis was not just a market phenomenon; it was deeply personal, affecting both Calamos staff and clients alike.

As clients bombarded the sales team with calls, fraught with worry about their accounts and the overall market stability, the team was under immense pressure to provide reassurance and clarity.

"Understandably, our clients were scared and worried," Waeyaert recounted. "They wanted to know what was happening with their investments, what John thought—given his decades of experience in the industry—and what our next moves were."

Amid this chaos, the sales team also grappled with concerns about their own job security and the firm's future. "Seeing other firms pull back or shut down, we couldn't help but worry about our own positions, and whether Calamos would still be around," Waeyaert explained.

"Knowledge helps beat fear. So we kept in touch regularly, bringing in our portfolio managers and investment pros to really break things down for our sales reps," said Waeyaert. This commitment to transparent and informed communication was crucial for guiding Calamos Investments through the stormy financial conditions.

The firm drove key messages that John had always emphasized: "staying invested is crucial as time in the market matters more than timing the market" and "focusing on the long term helps avoid rash decisions." These principles reflect John's belief in the resilience of the global economy, which, despite facing unprecedented challenges, has a consistent history of recovering and emerging stronger. By January 2009, the severity of the market meltdown made it clear that changes were inevitable. Despite the close-knit, family-like atmosphere at Calamos, the crisis forced John to make a difficult decision he had long avoided: layoffs.

Investment management is a high-margin business, enabling firms to weather some volatility in their revenue stream. However, the magnitude of the decline was so severe that many companies, including Calamos, could no longer survive without cutting staff.

Carla D'Antonio, vice president, Office of the Chairman, closely observed the strains and pressures that weighed heavily on John during the crisis. "It was a tense time," she recalled, noting the stressful atmosphere within the firm. "John and his leadership team were grappling with tough decisions to protect the firm."

Reflecting on that tough day, John recalled, "It was one of the hardest days; letting people go was necessary to keep us afloat, but it went against everything we stood for as a family at the firm."

The news of the layoffs spread rapidly, stirring a palpable sense of fear and uncertainty among the staff about potential further cuts. "The air was thick with worry—everyone was on edge, wondering if they would be next," Carla noted.

In response to the growing unease, John gathered the entire firm to communicate the harsh reality. "John's normal stoicism was shaken

113

that day, and I could see that he was struggling with the weight of delivering such bad news to people he cared so much about," Carla said. The emotional burden of laying off employees was a heavy one, especially for someone like John, who deeply valued his team.

"The room was heavy with emotion that day," Carla shared, recalling how even she couldn't help but feel moved by the somber mood. "It was one of the hardest things I've seen—watching John forced to make such a difficult decision, knowing how much it pained him."

Mae, who was also present during this moment, found it heart-wrenching to see John so emotional. "Trying to explain that these cuts were a necessary, albeit painful, step to stabilize the firm—it was heartbreaking," Mae shared, her voice heavy with emotion.

The first round of layoffs had been difficult, but as the crisis worsened, it became evident that further cuts were inevitable. This second wave, affecting an additional 50 employees, deeply affected the Calamos team, casting a shadow over the firm's morale.

As John outlined the dire situation and the measures taken, Mae stood in the back, tears streaming down her face. "I'll never forget it." She continued, "John stood there in front of everyone gathered in the cafeteria, just after we'd let another 50 employees go. He explained that it was critical to keep the firm afloat, to preserve jobs for the rest and ensure that Calamos didn't collapse under the crisis. Standing there, trying to hold the company together, you could see it weighed heavily on him."

Calamos laid off 102 employees, or just over 20% of their work-force, which at the time totaled 457. "It was one of the hardest things I've had to do," John shared, his voice reflecting the gravity of his decision.

During the financial crisis, John and his nephew, co-chief invest-ment officer Nick Calamos, took significant steps to support their team by reducing their own compensation. This reduction was not merely a personal sacrifice; it was a strategic decision aimed at supporting the bonus pool for the staff, ensuring that the team remained financially supported during the challenging period.

Shannon Hay, a member of John's communications team, emphasized the leadership's dedication during the financial crisis. "Even amid the turmoil, they did everything possible to prioritize us and ensure our families' well-being," she noted.

This was just one of many instances she witnessed that exemplified John's leadership style and his commitment to the firm's "family." "That's just who John is," she remarked, underscoring the deep level of care and responsibility John felt toward his employees.

Reflecting on the financial crisis, John shared how the turmoil reshaped Calamos Investments' strategic direction. "Market fluctuations are always really based on what is happening in the world around you," John explained.

The scale and suddenness of the 2008 crisis demanded an adaptive response unlike any before. "It alerted us to the need for a broader perspective," John explained. In response, he focused on understanding the needs of investors outside the United States while also enhancing resources to seize opportunities in international markets.

"We wanted to expand our reach, so we dedicated more energy to assembling a team focused on overseas markets, not just US markets," he detailed. This strategic shift addressed immediate challenges and set Calamos Investments on a new trajectory.

The lessons learned during these tumultuous times reinforced the resilience of Calamos Investments, emphasizing perseverance and a focus on long-term goals. Hillenbrand highlighted the firm's resilience during the crisis, noting the tangible results: "The proof point came in 2009 when two of our largest funds significantly outperformed."

He further underscored the consistent portfolio strategy adopted by the firm, stating, "We were trying to strike that balance—gaining upside potential while being mindful of the volatility." Conclusively, he remarked, "The fact that we performed well on the way out shows that we weren't caught flat-footed," emphasizing the firm's adept handling of the crisis.

"We practiced what we preached," John reflected, "maintaining our focus on the long term, which is crucial in understanding that both the economy and the markets can weather unprecedented storms and emerge stronger."

This period not only underscored the resilience of the entire Calamos team but also reaffirmed John's commitment to exceptional client service and continuous innovation, principles that guided Calamos through the storm and toward a stronger future.

Chapter 18

A New Era Begins

In 2013, still grappling with the aftermath of the 2008 financial crisis, Calamos Investments was immersed in a dynamic phase of global expansion and product diversification despite facing challenges like net outflows and declining revenues.

Although many smaller boutique firms had been absorbed by larger entities, Calamos stood out as a rare example of an independent firm that had maintained its autonomy and continued on its own path of growth, bucking the trend seen among its competitors.

However, amid this complex backdrop, John found the dual demands of his roles as chief executive officer and chief investment officer increasingly untenable, particularly as the company expanded. Recognizing the need to preserve the stability of the company and establish a lasting legacy, he began to prioritize succession planning to ensure a seamless transition in leadership for the future as the company expanded.

He realized he needed to focus on what he does best—investment management—to effectively tackle ongoing challenges in the aftermath of the largest financial crisis since the Great Depression.

This insight led him to seriously consider handing over the chief executive officer role—a position he had held since founding the firm in 1977. This would free him to concentrate on improving investment performance. He believed this shift would help steady the firm and line up its operations with its long-term goals of expanding globally and excelling in client service—even if it meant giving up the helm of the company bearing his own name.

"It became clear that managing both the investment side and the operational side was too much. While I'm an investment guy at heart, I was trying to be a CEO and I don't think I did as good a job of that, quite frankly." This humility highlighted his pragmatic approach to leadership—acknowledging his strengths in investment strategy over daily corporate management.

"I needed to focus where I could add the most value. It's always been about how we're performing for our clients," John said, emphasizing his commitment to client outcomes.

That same year, John's nephew, Nick Calamos, decided to depart the firm to devote more time to his nonprofit and charitable interests. He was succeeded by a seasoned executive to serve as a global co-chief investment officer, however, the relationship lasted less than three years, illustrating the complexities of filling C-suite positions within an established corporate culture.

John has always believed in the importance of a skilled and dedicated team. "It's really all about the people you have, how you bring them in, and what they can do," he remarked. This philosophy extended beyond the executive offices and influenced the entire organization.

With this in mind, John made a strategic decision to bring in someone who could excel at attracting and managing talent, enabling him to focus on his broader responsibilities while also initiating a succession plan. It was during John's deep reflection on these topics that he crossed paths with John Koudounis. Both men embodied the ethos of the American Dream.

Koudounis mirrored John's entrepreneurial spirit and shared deep ties to Chicago's Greek community. Like John, his family had immigrated from Greece and embraced the promise of the American Dream. His father was a small business owner, and his parents were deeply committed to encouraging their children's academic achievements. Koudounis was the first male in his family to attend college, going to the prestigious Brown University.

Koudounis carved out a path of self-made success. His early career steps included an elite internship at Merrill Lynch, reflecting a work ethic and a trajectory similar to John's, where education and determination opened doors to new opportunities. Both were also active in philanthropy and deeply involved in their local Hellenic community, underscoring their commitment to giving back and fostering community ties.

Koudounis's introduction to Calamos Investments traced back to his early career with Merril Lynch in the late 1980s, a time when Calamos's financial products began carving out significant space in the industry.

"Throughout my career, my teams and colleagues frequently engaged with Calamos offerings," Koudounis shared, highlighting the respect he had for John's expansive influence. Although he didn't deal much with John or his firm directly back then, he was well aware of the widespread reputation Calamos had built before they ever met personally.

Koudounis was president and CEO of Mizuho Securities USA Inc. During his time at Mizuho, he transformed the firm into a full-service investment bank by expanding its debt and equity capital markets teams. Koudounis's path to Calamos Investments started unexpectedly against the backdrop of his busy travel routine.

His responsibilities spanned across multiple continents from Tokyo to London, and a routine that had him flying from Chicago to New York weekly.

"It all started when my assistant received a call," Koudounis recounted. "She said, 'There's a Mr. John Calamos who wants to meet with you.' And I remember thinking, really? The John Calamos?"

His curiosity was piqued. As they tried to coordinate a meeting, the challenge of Koudounis's travel-heavy role became apparent. "I was constantly on the move, mostly airborne, barely at home except on weekends to be with my wife and twin daughters," he explained.

After some back and forth, it became clear that finding a mutual time to meet in New York wouldn't work due to John's schedule being tied to the Chicago area. "I realized I wouldn't be in Chicago for work for another two and a half months," Koudounis said.

However, an opportunity arose for a brief return home. "My assistant clarified that I'd be in Chicago for just 48 hours over a weekend." Despite the brevity of his time in Chicago, Koudounis arranged for an early Saturday morning breakfast with John in Naperville. "It can be an hour and a half drive, but I was more than happy to make it for the chance to meet John," he noted.

At first, Koudounis wasn't sure what the meeting was about, but he quickly became engaged in a rich conversation that flowed between personal anecdotes and career achievements, enhanced by their shared experiences growing up in Chicagoland's tightly knit Greek American community.

"To be honest, I didn't have any specific expectations beyond just meeting John. But I quickly realized this could lead to something more substantial," Koudounis reflected on the encounter.

"I've been hearing a lot about you. You're active in the Greek community, from Chicago, and you have a solid footing in the business community here. I figured we ought to meet," John expressed, acknowledging the influence of their shared connections.

As they spoke, it became clear that John was contemplating a role of some sort for Koudounis at Calamos Investments. The discussion subtly shifted to evaluating potential business synergies, particularly concerning Koudounis's expertise in investment banking and his ability to navigate complex market dynamics.

John, impressed by Koudounis's recent feature profile in *Forbes Magazine* and his proven leadership track record, recognized the ideal qualities for the leadership role he envisioned. John began involving Koudounis in activities that promoted their shared commitment to advancing Hellenic values and philanthropy, fostering a friendship that opened doors for Koudounis to build new connections with leaders at local, national, and global levels. Koudounis expressed his gratitude for these opportunities, noting, "I'm deeply thankful to John for welcoming me into these high-level experiences, which have been really eye-opening and rewarding."

Despite this growing camaraderie, it would be a few more years before any professional collaboration materialized.

As John reflected on his decision to hire a CEO, he acknowledged that he considered various candidates before John Koudounis, mainly chief investment officers who could take on greater responsibility. However, he found that many of these candidates lacked the robust management focus critical to his company's needs.

"I realized as I reflected upon the successes of leading CEOs in the investment industry—people like Larry Fink of BlackRock and Jamie Dimon of JPMorgan Chase—what made them exceptional leaders was their focus on effective business management, rather than just investments," John explained. "Seeing how they operated really opened my eyes to the importance of having a CEO who could streamline our business operations instead of getting bogged down in the minute points of our investment strategies."

John believed that Koudounis's combination of investment expertise and his success in navigating the complexities of a major financial institution equipped him with the ideal skills for a CEO. "Despite some initial resistance from my team, who were likely

121

A New Era Begins

cautious about changes in the reporting structure," John remarked, "I was struck by Koudounis's impressive blend of investment knowledge and management prowess, which clearly distinguished him as the perfect choice for CEO."

John proceeded with his plan, believing that restructuring the company's top management was essential for its future growth. When Koudounis officially joined Calamos Investments, his appointment came as a surprise to many in the company. Calamos noted, "It was a bit of a shock because it really was about reorganizing the business at the top level."

Koudounis, with his engaging personality and proactive approach, didn't waste any time aligning the team with the company's new direction. He instituted twice weekly meetings to foster open communication and ensure that all team members felt included and informed.

"He did a good job of getting the group together and maintaining open lines of communication," said John, appreciating Koudounis's efforts to integrate and lead the team effectively.

The transition wasn't just about changing personnel but also redefining how the company operated at its core, with John focusing on partnering with a leader whose strengths complemented his own.

As John transitioned to a more strategic role within the company, he noted, "It's incredibly beneficial to have a CEO with a fresh perspective. John [Koudounis] has brought in some exceptional individuals, particularly in management roles."

This positive impression was pivotal in John's decision to bring Koudounis on board, believing he could introduce new vitality into the company. Their work together quickly turned into a meaningful friendship, enriched by shared experiences and their backgrounds and values.

Now serving as chairman and global chief investment officer, John focuses on guiding board decisions and collaborating on setting the strategic direction of the company. His role involves a careful balance of oversight and visionary leadership, ensuring that the company not only maintains its course but also adapts and thrives in an ever-changing financial landscape.

Chapter 19

Reclaiming Control

Following the tumultuous period of the 2008 financial crisis—a global downturn that tested the resilience of financial institutions worldwide—John found himself reassessing the strategic direction of his company. In the aftermath of the crisis, the regulatory environment for public companies intensified significantly, bringing with it a wave of challenging regulations.

Although John understood the necessity of rules to ensure fairness in the market, he was critical of the overly burdensome regulations that emerged. "We found ourselves entangled in red tape, purportedly to protect shareholder values, yet it hampered our ability to innovate and serve our clients effectively," he noted.

He expressed frustration over the excessive regulatory environment, which sapped resources and attention: "Rather than focusing on our core mission of serving clients, we were swamped with filling out forms and preparing repetitive paperwork."

This era highlighted the increasing complexity of the global economy, complicating the task of identifying risks. "Navigating these complexities demanded a steadfast focus on the investment landscape, a task that was continually undermined by external pressures," John observed.

His thoughts captured the tension between meeting regulatory demands and pursuing the firm's strategic objectives, illustrating the significant challenges the firm faced as it sought to recalibrate its growth trajectory during a critical period.

During this time, the company also experienced management changes, which reflected broader industry trends where leadership turnover increased as firms sought new strategies to navigate the post-crisis landscape.

Amid the complexities of maintaining shareholder satisfaction, the operational hurdles of being a publicly traded company, and the strategic necessity for agility in a changing economic environment, John started to consider the advantages of taking the company private.

John saw this move as a strategy to regain control and refocus the company away from the insatiable appetite for short-term performance from public investors toward long-term stability and growth.

"The constant scrutiny for scrutiny's sake, and the need to meet short-term financial targets were becoming too much," he explained. "With our stock undervalued and business activities stifled, it seemed like the perfect moment to transition back to private ownership and reorganize the company for future growth."

Once convinced of his decision, John confided in his CEO, John Koudounis, to thoughtfully and thoroughly discuss the timing and benefits of proposing a public buyback. Koudounis understood John's frustration with the constraints of public ownership, sparking the first of several discussions. He supported the move, recalling their talks on the operational challenges and necessary strategic adjustments. "I agreed with John, to restore the company to a position of strength, we need to go private to secure the freedom necessary for effective growth."

Going public initially offered many promising prospects for the company, but over time, the disadvantages began to outweigh the benefits. The discussions in the boardroom, instead of being lively Socratic debates aimed at challenging the status quo, fell short of John's expectations for innovation and improvement.

"John wasn't used to answering to anyone other than his clients. This fiduciary duty has always been core to his identity," Koudounis added. "And suddenly, he was accountable to shareholders, too."

The decision to go private wasn't taken lightly. It was a carefully thought-out move to reclaim control over the company's destiny, streamline operations, and focus more on client relations and growth. Koudounis emphasized the importance of having experienced leadership during this transition. "Staying the course, believing in what you do, was really important," he noted, underscoring the confidence that John's leadership instilled in both investors and employees during turbulent times.

Koudounis's role in steering the company through these changes was critical. His leadership as CEO helped maintain stability and investor confidence, proving that sometimes, the best way to protect a vision is to shield it from public pressures and focus on what made the company successful in the first place: innovation, client-centric strategies, and a dedicated team.

"Going private wasn't just to avoid the difficulties of being a public company; it was to start a new chapter for Calamos Investments, focused on growth and innovation," Koudounis said, highlighting how important this decision was.

On Monday December 19, 2016, John Calamos and John Koudounis executed on their strategic move to privatize the company, announcing a tender offer of $8.25 per share. This offer represented a significant 12% premium over the closing stock price of $7.36 from the previous Friday, underscoring their commitment to reclaim and revitalize the company.

This announcement sent shares rising sharply to $8.39 by mid-day, a robust 14% increase, as shareholders anticipated an even richer final deal.

On January 11, 2017, Calamos Asset Management Inc. sealed its transition back to a private company. This change was driven by a vision to prioritize long-term strategic goals over the fleeting demands of market fluctuations.

The buyback was meticulously structured through the tender offer in cash for all outstanding Class A shares, concluding with a second-step merger for any remaining shares at the identical rate. This carefully executed process, which began within a week of the agreement, received full endorsement from both the board and an independent special committee, and was set to complete in the first quarter.

In this moment, John found himself steering his company once more, relishing the return to its roots. He felt lighter, more agile, and deeply connected to his entrepreneurial spirit—a transition that was both profound and deeply personal. This strategic pivot enabled him to pursue a broader range of investment opportunities and refine the company's focus.

His leadership during this transition was marked by a deliberate and thoughtful approach, underscored by his commitment to the company's long-term strategic goals. Reflecting on the experience, he explains that transitioning to a public company wasn't inherently detrimental, but its success hinged significantly on the company's specific context and its capacity for management. He advised, "Going public isn't a bad idea per se, but it really depends on the company and where it's headed."

John specifically criticized the traditional corporate governance model that's become prevalent in many public companies. "You get too caught up in making the board and shareholders happy, and you lose sight of what really matters—making the whole company and our clients happy."

For Calamos Investments, the next chapter would be written based on John's wisdom, foresight, and dedication to his clients—not by the priorities of investors only interested in the next quarter's financials.

Chapter 20

From Success to Significance

John's life journey has reflected many of the ideals set forth by Socrates. He started as an eager student, then proudly served his country, and later built Calamos Investments into a global asset manager. Now, with the firm established, John focused more on making a broad, lasting impact. For him, being a statesman wasn't about entering politics; it was about nurturing and defending democratic ideals through civic engagement and philanthropy. It reflects his belief that true leadership involves giving back and uplifting others, ensuring that the lessons he's learned along the way continue to inspire future generations.

Another motivating factor for John is his realization that he has achieved what once seemed like a distant dream—the American Dream. His rise to great heights in the financial world is even more inspirational considering his humble early beginnings.

In 2004, John established The John P. Calamos Foundation, formalizing his commitment to philanthropy. This foundation embodies the deeply held values that John and Mae share, reflecting their dedication to giving back and supporting meaningful causes.

The foundation supports a wide array of initiatives that are important to them, including honoring military service members and veterans, leadership development, entrepreneurship and education, philosophy as a tool for self-knowledge, financial literacy, and the preservation and advancement of Hellenic heritage and culture.

It also plays a significant role in the Naperville, Illinois, community and surrounding areas by backing various civic and community-based initiatives. This commitment demonstrates their vision of making a lasting, positive impact on society while upholding their core values.

One of John and Mae's most significant philanthropic efforts was their generous multimillion-dollar donation to Illinois Tech in 2011, an institution that John credits with fundamentally shaping his character and career. Through The John P. Calamos Foundation, they established two endowed chairs: the Stuart School of Business Dean Endowed Chair and the institution's first Endowed Chair in Philosophy.

John explained the motivation behind their gift of a philosophy chair in a school especially well known for subjects like business and engineering: "Supporting Illinois Tech is not just about giving back; it's about investing in the future leaders who will drive innovation and uphold the values we cherish. Mae and I saw this contribution as a way to strengthen the foundation of education and critical thinking that profoundly changed my life."

J. D. Trout, the John & Mae Calamos Endowed Chair in Philosophy, provides deeper insights into what drives John's philanthropy. "I have often wondered about John's strong connection to Illinois Tech," Professor Trout reflects. "After spending time with him, I believe it boils down to two cherished values: his heritage and his deep attachment to philosophy. John's background—not only as a Greek American but also as someone who started from humble beginnings—profoundly influences him."

Professor Trout continued, "The chair's endowment transforms a simple departmental professor into a kind of ambassador for research and teaching throughout the university. All of this is possible because John has an enterprising generosity towards young people who are trying to launch promising careers, just as he did."

John reflected on his decision to endow a chair in philosophy, a subject that significantly influenced his academic and professional paths. "During my time at Illinois Tech, transitioning from architecture to finance, the critical thinking skills I developed were life-changing," he explained. "My education was crucial to my success over the years," John noted, emphasizing the lasting influence of his philosophy classes. "It's essential for me that future business students understand how profoundly philosophy can impact their careers."

In May 2022, Illinois Tech invited John to deliver the commencement address. During his speech, he shared his personal journey: "Illinois Tech is renowned for its academic rigor, but what I truly valued was the freedom to explore a wide range of subjects. This interdisciplinary approach not only broadened my understanding of the world but also clarified my path in it."

Building on his commitment to education, John further solidified his legacy at Illinois Tech in 2024 with a substantial contribution aimed at expanding financial aid for students and ensuring the institution's long-term stability.

His donation was met with profound gratitude, as expressed by Illinois Tech president Raj Echambadi in a board letter: "We're humbled by John's selfless act of generosity and his inspiring commitment to fuel opportunity for many thousands of present and future Illinois Tech students."

John's contributions reflect his dedication to creating opportunities for the next generation. His ongoing support continues to shape Illinois Tech's mission, ensuring that students from modest backgrounds, like himself, have access to a quality education and the resources they need to succeed.

In addition to their contributions to Illinois Tech, John and Mae have actively promoted Greek heritage through their involvement with the National Hellenic Museum in Chicago. This museum connects generations with Greek history, culture, and art, embodying John's heritage and core values. It celebrates the legacy of Hellenism and the contributions of Greek immigrants and Greek Americans, ensuring that the principles of democracy, philosophy, and innovation continue to inspire future generations.

John's initial motivation to become involved with the museum was to honor his parents. To that end, he joined the museum's board and played a key role in its relocation to a new site, with support from then-mayor Richard M. Daley. Daley helped arrange the relocation of a business previously on the museum's current site and facilitated financing through the establishment of a tax increment financing district, underscoring his support for Chicago's Greek community.

As the museum transitioned into the new building, John's role evolved; he was appointed chairman of the board. Under his leadership, the museum not only celebrated Greek heritage locally but also expanded its mission nationally, engaging the broader Greek community across the United States.

John viewed the museum as an essential educational tool for young people to understand Greek heritage, again recalling the sentiment, "You don't know where you're going unless you know where you came from."

Marianne Kountoures, executive director of the National Hellenic Museum, describes it as "more than a repository of history; it is a vibrant place, continually enriched by John's robust support, for people of all ages and backgrounds who want to understand the compelling story of the Greek people and their contributions to humanity."

She emphasizes that John's contributions go beyond financial support; he brings innovative ideas, recruits new team members, and provides resources that enhance the museum's appeal across generations and cultures.

"John has embraced Hellenic ideals such as service, civility, and commitment to family and community," Marianne observes. "These principles guide his life and are integral to his mission of inspiring future generations." She emphasizes his proactive approach: "He leads by example, never asking others to do something he wouldn't do himself, reflecting how deeply his heritage shapes his actions."

John's passion for the museum's potential remains strong, even as he faces the challenge of engaging a digitally distracted generation. He believes deeply in the enriching power of heritage, especially for young people.

To make Greek culture more relevant, the museum has launched dynamic initiatives, including standout projects like the National Hellenic Museum Trial Series, which presents historical hearings, such as Socrates's prosecution for allegedly corrupting Athens's youth.

These trials are designed to revive critical moments in Greek history and spark lively discussions among attendees, applying modern day legal arguments to ancient topics and characters. "We held these trials to spark interest in Greek history and provoke thoughtful discussion," John explained, underscoring the intention behind these vivid mock trials with seasoned lawyers arguing the case anew.

In its "2024 Trial of Pericles," the museum staged a trial to debate whether Pericles, who played a pivotal role in the development of democracy about 500 BCE, was a tyrant or a hero. "It's a way to make history tangible and engaging for the next generation," John added, highlighting his commitment to educational innovation at the museum.

The events, featuring prominent local judges and attorneys and engaging hundreds of students, included jury decisions and audience participation. "The audience gets involved, too, weighing in on the historical verdicts," John explained.

Attendees used colored cards to cast their verdicts, adding an interactive element to the trials that spurred great interest from the general public, reinforcing John's dedication to preserving cultural heritage and engaging communities.

This same commitment to faith and heritage was evident in his significant donation to support the rebuilding of the Saint Nicholas Greek Orthodox Church and National Shrine at Ground Zero, destroyed on 9/11. The new church, designed by architect Santiago Calatrava and inspired by Byzantine architecture and landmarks like the Hagia Sophia and the Parthenon, was conceived as both a place of worship and a symbol of hope and unity.

"I donated to the Saint Nicholas National Shrine to ensure future generations have the same opportunity to connect with their faith," John said, highlighting the importance of preserving spiritual and cultural heritage. John's contribution to the church's reconstruction reflects his deep belief in the power of faith and community. "This church isn't just a building; it's a lasting symbol of resilience that I hope inspires future generations," he said.

His commitment to bringing history to life for young people is just one aspect of his broader philanthropic vision. "I want to make meaningful connections through my work," John explained.

While he supports education, Hellenic culture, and the arts, he has a particular dedication to honoring veterans, especially those who served in Vietnam and faced a cold and even hostile reception on returning home. "These brave individuals deserve our recognition and respect," he emphasizes, demonstrating his unwavering dedication to service and community.

John's commitment is exemplified by his involvement with the Distinguished Flying Cross Society—an honor he himself received—which underscores his deep passion for aviation and the profound impact military service has had on his life.

Additionally, he honors heroism through his support for The Washington Oxi Day Foundation, which celebrates Greek bravery in conflicts from World War II to the present. By recognizing the courage and sacrifices of Greek service members across generations, the organization ensures their legacy of service is remembered and celebrated today. Reflecting on John's influence on The Washington Oxi Day Foundation, executive director Mike Manatos describes him as "the epitome of impactful philanthropy," highlighting the respect and gratitude he has garnered within the community.

John was the first Vietnam veteran to receive the Jaharis Service Award from the Oxi Day Foundation, honoring his extensive community service. Following this recognition, the foundation, with John's support, established the Calamos Service Award. This annual honor recognizes a Greek American Vietnam veteran for their dedicated service and contributions to the United States and the world, embodying John's spirit and commitment to honoring those who have served.

Manatos emphasizes the significance of John's contributions, stating, "John's leadership and generosity have been instrumental not only in honoring our veterans but also in preserving and enriching our community's narrative through the National Hellenic Museum and other initiatives. His efforts solidify our collective identity and deepen our historical understanding."

In 2015, John's commitment to preserving Greek heritage took center stage once again with a significant donation from his foundation to bring *The Greeks: Agamemnon to Alexander the Great* exhibit to Chicago's Field Museum.

This exhibit, a partnership between the Field Museum and the National Hellenic Museum—where John served as chairman of the board of trustees—showcased over 500 priceless artifacts from 21 Greek museums, many of which were displayed outside Greece for the first time.

John expressed pride in cosponsoring the exhibition, saying, "The National Hellenic Museum is the premier Greek cultural institution in North America, and it's a privilege to support an exhibit that highlights the pivotal contributions of ancient Greece to democracy and Western culture."

The exhibit, along with companion programs hosted at the National Hellenic Museum, offered visitors a deep dive into 5,000 years of Greek history. "This wasn't just about artifacts," John noted. "It was about connecting people to a culture that shaped so much of the modern world."

This initiative further underscores John's dedication to preserving and promoting Greek history, ensuring its lessons and legacy continue to inspire future generations. Their commitment to Greek heritage aligns seamlessly with John and Mae's broader philanthropic ethos, which emphasizes education, heritage, and valor.

"Giving back, especially in this phase of my life, is crucial," John emphasized. Mae echoed this sentiment: "We aim not just to support with funds but to actively engage in causes that promote education and civic values, hoping to inspire others to do the same."

John and Mae aspire for the Calamos name to embody generosity and civic engagement. "We want our legacy to resonate for years to come, enhancing lives and encouraging others to contribute positively to society," John said.

Chapter 21

Global Influence

In 2011, Greece faced a severe financial crisis that played a significant role in the broader economic difficulties affecting the eurozone. This period was marked by extreme economic instability in Greece, as the country struggled with crippling debt, skyrocketing unemployment, and strict austerity measures from international creditors. These policies led to widespread public unrest and a pervasive sense of despair among the populace.

The Greek government was under intense pressure to implement harsh fiscal reforms and spending cuts to qualify for bailout funds from the European Union and the International Monetary Fund. These measures, however, led to a deep recession, compounding the already dire economic conditions and fueling public outrage against both the Greek government and its international lenders.

John had long harbored an affection for his family's ancestral homeland, actively maintaining relationships with Greek governmental leaders and like-minded business figures concerned about Greece's future. Amid this severe crisis, John's connection to Greece earned him an invitation to speak at the pivotal Greek Power Summit 2011: Helping Greece Rebuild, organized by Honeystone Ltd., Cyprus & UK, the publishers of the Greek *Rich List Magazine*, and the international consultancy firm, IAC. This conference was dedicated to addressing the nation's economic challenges.

The summit attracted a diverse group of participants from sectors such as shipping, finance, technology, banking, and tourism, encompassing both public and private spheres. As the head of a leading global asset management firm, John was sought for his economic expertise and insights, alongside influential figures like Steve Forbes and various leaders from Europe, Australia, and beyond.

This gathering aimed to harness collective wisdom to navigate Greece through its crisis by drawing on advice and strategies from a mix of Greek and international experts. John traveled to the summit with Mae, as well as two generations of their blended family, including a number of their grandchildren. Also joining them was Calamos Investments chief of staff Yanni Sianis.

Although the trip was primarily for business, the journey was deeply personal for John, echoing the previous visit with his father that had been profoundly meaningful. John wanted to deepen his family's connection to their heritage by exposing them to Greece's natural beauty, ancient architecture, and the warmth of its people. His hope was that this journey would let them experience firsthand the rich history and vibrant culture, helping them better understand and appreciate his ancestral roots.

On arriving at Parliament Square in Athens, the severity of the crisis was glaringly obvious right outside their accommodations at the Hotel Grande Bretagne. Yanni vividly recalled the chaotic scene: "The air was thick with smoke from Molotov cocktails, stinging our nostrils, and we had to wear masks to breathe. Protesters were tearing apart the stone steps in front of our hotel, turning the fragments into makeshift weapons. Cars were set ablaze throughout the area." Adding poignancy, he noted, "This was hardly the introduction to Greece that John had envisioned for his family's visit."

As John prepared to speak at the conference, the tensions outside increased significantly. "The day I was scheduled to speak, there were numerous protests, including some right outside our hotel conference room," John recalled. The unrest escalated to the point where hotel security had to use underground passages to safely escort John and other attendees between meetings and other events.

The discussions at the summit, primarily with European leaders, focused intensely on Greece's crippling debt burden, which dominated the agenda for potential solutions. John viewed his role at the summit as a staunch advocate for reducing bureaucratic barriers and encouraging foreign investment.

"Cut the red tape, roll out the red carpet, and you'll attract investments," John emphasized, critiquing Greece's stringent regulatory measures and their restrictive impact on economic growth. Highlighting the extent of bureaucratic overreach, John offered a compelling example of how restrictive policies not only drive away international investment but also stifle small business owners: "There was this case of a bookstore owner who wanted to add a small coffee shop to his store. It took him two years just to secure the necessary permits."

Building on his advocacy for small businesses, John emphasized their crucial role in the US economy as engines of job creation. Reflecting on his own journey, he shared, "My road to the American Dream began with my family's grocery store, followed by my ventures into small businesses and eventually growing Calamos into a global firm."

His message was strong and clear—the governments of Greece and Europe needed to make it easier to do business in the country. Surrounded by journalists at one of these discussions, John openly criticized the lack of media coverage on the necessary economic reforms. Frustrated with the passive media response, he challenged the reporters, "Why don't we see something about that in the newspaper?" As the discussion grew more heated, John recalled, "I pride myself on being in control, but I couldn't let it stand. It was just too important of a point—government policy and fiscal policy set the stage for the prosperity or poverty of individuals, households, businesses, and entire economies."

As John prepared to leave the event, he had a telling exchange with a reporter that shed light on the restrictive media environment. The reporter confided, "Mr. Calamos, we are essentially muzzled by government ownership; we can't freely express our views," highlighting the substantial challenges journalists faced in advocating for change.

This incident highlighted the daunting challenges John encountered while advocating for change in a system where government control stifles the media, curbing free speech and critical reporting.

Reflecting on the experience, John asserted, "For a society to truly flourish, a free and vibrant press is essential, with minimal government interference in both the marketplace and public discourse."

John's commitment to ethical business practices is deeply rooted in his leadership experience, where he has seen firsthand the importance of transparency and fair regulations. He emphasizes, "These principles are not just good policy; they are critical for success in both business and governance."

John's steadfast belief in the resilience of societies to overcome economic and social challenges is deeply influenced by his understanding of Greek philosophy and culture. Drawing from the philosophical insights he gained in college, John maintains a hopeful outlook even in difficult times. He believes that human ingenuity and innovation can help us navigate through unprecedented challenges.

Moreover, like many Greeks, he holds a profound appreciation for the power of a strong work ethic, considering it essential for curing many societal ills. This blend of cultural heritage and philosophical insight fueled his optimism for Greece's ability to surmount its challenges and emerge stronger.

John reflected on the participation of various Greek government factions at the summit, observing their strong presence, particularly from conservative sectors. "They were notably receptive to our discussions on reforms, aligning well with their advocacy for fiscal responsibility and structural changes," he noted.

John emphasized the importance of leveraging Greece's competitive advantages to revitalize its economy. "Focusing on key sectors like shipping and tourism, which Greece excels in, is crucial for economic stability and growth," he stated. He underscored the significance of tourism in attracting international visitors and generating substantial revenue, highlighting how countries, like businesses, thrive by capitalizing on their unique strengths.

John observed that the chaotic scenes—smoke filling the streets and rocks hurled through the air—were hardly the backdrop to attract tourists to Greece's rich history and beauty. He reflected on the impact of political leadership on economic stability, noting, "Economic success fluctuates with governance, just like in any country, depending on who's in charge."

John observed significant strategic shifts in Greece's government priorities, notably the emphasis on strengthening the tourism sector to stabilize the economy. He highlighted the crucial link between effective leadership and targeted economic strategies. "Effective political leadership and strategic economic policies are essential for shaping fiscal health," he explained.

Since 2011, Greece's economy transitioned from a severe crisis, characterized by recession and high unemployment, to a period of recovery marked by strong employment growth, increased investment, and rising exports, supported by government measures like the National Recovery & Resistance Plan ("Greece 2.0"). However, John noted, "Despite positive changes, ongoing economic challenges, such as rising energy costs and global uncertainties, continue to temper the pace of recovery."

When it was time to leave the summit, Yanni recounted the measures taken to ensure safety amid the escalating chaos. "We were guided through a secret tunnel that led to a secondary building where a car was waiting to quickly take us away from the rioting," he explained.

As the protests grew more intense, John couldn't shake his worry for Mae and the kids while they explored Athens. He and Mae had been closely following reports and had decided that some modest sightseeing would still be okay, reflecting their confidence in the hospitality and kindness of the Greek people.

Unfortunately, conditions deteriorated unexpectedly, but their view of the citizens of Athens proved correct. Mae described their experience running through the streets to escape a sudden volley of tear gas. "A kind gentleman opened the door to his restaurant, ushering us in and said, 'Stay, you're safe here,' providing us with wet napkins to cover our faces and protect us from the smoke."

After these events, John felt a wave of relief when one of his young grandchildren thanked him and Mae for the time spent together as a family. Calling him by the Greek word for grandfather, he exclaimed, "Papou, that was the best trip ever!" They were thrilled to see the places John had often described from his ancestral homeland come to life.

The Greek Power Summit 2011, despite the surrounding turmoil, provided a vital platform for serious discussions about Greece's economic revival, with John passionately advocating for major regulatory reforms. John continued to lend his voice and business experience to help Greece, including by participating in the 2012 summit hosted by The Hellenic Initiative and led by former US president Bill Clinton.

At the summit, the Greek prime minister unveiled an ambitious plan to cut through the bureaucratic red tape that had been stifling the economy and making Greece less inviting to investors. John, as a board member, and John Koudounis, a founding board member and executive committee member, were instrumental in shaping these discussions.

The proposed reforms—aimed at enhancing the private sector, encouraging business building and entrepreneurship, freeing up capital markets, ensuring effective government oversight, and maintaining equitable taxation—promised to revitalize the economy by fostering innovation and creativity.

This approach mirrored strategies that had driven growth in developed markets like the United States, suggesting that these principles could help fulfill the "Greek Dream," much like they enabled the Calamos family and other immigrants to achieve the American Dream.

John's commitment to Greece's well-being remains steadfast. Through the smoke of conflict and the corridors of crisis, his dedication to advocate for meaningful economic reforms and inspire resilience shone brightly.

In every measure he advocated, John's resolve was clear: to support and uplift his ancestral homeland, embodying a hopeful spirit that one day, Greece would flourish again, thanks to its own determination and efforts and the support of its global community and allies.

Chapter 22

Excellence, Innovation, and Leadership

A quote often attributed to Aristotle says, "We are what we repeatedly do. Excellence, then, is not an act, but a habit."

By the early 2000s, the market provided the perfect stage for John and his firm to put this philosophy into action as they constantly sought new ways to innovate for their clients. Their success was no accident; it resulted from careful preparation, foresight, and an unwavering commitment to continuous improvement.

"We brought in more people to focus on technology, enhancing our strategies with quantitative analysis," John explained. This forward-thinking emphasis on data-driven markets not only helped navigate the ups and downs in the markets but also laid the groundwork for Calamos's long-term success, positioning the firm to thrive in an ever-evolving financial landscape.

In 2002, amid ongoing market fluctuations, Calamos launched the first of several multi-asset convertible closed-end funds, capitalizing on the advantages of their unique structure. "The market had taken a downturn around 2001, and convertibles were trading well below what we saw as fair value," he recalled.

In these closed-end funds, John's approach involved blending stocks, bonds, and convertibles to offer income with reduced exposure to interest rate risk, setting his funds apart from traditional fixed-income options. "Closed-end funds can achieve many asset allocation goals, including long-term capital growth and stable income," John explained.

To meet investor needs, he developed an innovative strategy that tapped into the high-income potential of temporarily distressed convertible securities, which were offering attractively high yields. "Market dislocations create real opportunities for long-term investors, and that's our focus," John said.

Seizing this moment, he launched a closed-end fund in 2002 designed to provide both high income and total return, giving investors a way to benefit from these undervalued assets. The success of John's first closed-end fund demonstrated his knack for understanding market needs. "We started with one fund focused on income, and after its success, we launched others with different areas of emphasis, but always aimed at serving income-oriented investors," John shared. "Now, we manage seven of these closed-end funds."

In 2004, Calamos Investments launched the largest closed-end fund of its time, showcasing the firm's ability to navigate market challenges and seize unique investment opportunities. This achievement reflects the company's talent for thriving in changing environments while consistently meeting investor needs.

"John has always been that kind of innovator," shared Scott Becker, senior vice president and senior portfolio specialist, who has worked with John for over 20 years. Scott emphasized that John's approach is rooted in a deep understanding of client needs and market opportunities.

The firm's product rollouts aren't random; they are "natural extensions of the capabilities we've already built, aligned with what investors need as global capital markets evolve."

Innovation, combined with relentless hard work, has been central to the firm's success, and John has led that charge every step of the way.

After managing money for institutional investors overseas for years, John took a new step in 2007 by launching UCITS Funds (Undertakings for Collective Investment in Transferable Securities).

This move opened the door for non-US investors to access Calamos's strategies, giving them a chance to benefit from the firm's expertise.

John always had a global vision, but expanding internationally meant he had to adapt and learn about new markets. He was well aware of the challenges of operating in Europe, especially when it came to navigating the complexities of different governments and regulatory frameworks.

Understanding the intricacies of European markets was only the beginning. "European markets come with their own set of challenges," John explained. "It's more complicated because you're dealing with various governments." Despite these hurdles, his firm's experience and flexible strategies enabled them to manage risks effectively and drive global growth.

However, regulatory knowledge alone wasn't enough to make a real impact. Expanding into Europe wasn't just about navigating the regulatory landscape; it meant hitting the road and meeting investment professionals across the continent. John personally engaged with potential investors, sharing the Calamos story while gaining insights into the unique needs and challenges of these markets.

Scott Becker recalls these meetings with John as some of the most intense yet inspiring experiences of his career. "John is definitely a roll-up-the-sleeves, hands-on kind of guy," Scott says. "He's always committed to real dialogue. Every market is different, so while he was eager to share what Calamos does, he was just as excited to learn and better understand the needs of each client."

These meetings, often organized with a private bank in Geneva, Switzerland, aimed to introduce Calamos funds and asset management services to a global clientele. "We'd do these at least once a year, if not more, and the schedule was intense," Scott recalls.

He describes the fast pace—landing in a city late in the evening, jumping into a dinner meeting with a local relationship team, catching just a few hours of sleep, and then diving into a full day of back-to-back meetings. By evening, they'd be on to the next city or even another country, ready to start the cycle all over again.

Despite the demanding pace, the international teams always greeted them warmly and went out of their way to showcase the best of their cities. Even in his seventies, John never missed a beat. Scott recalls how their hosts would sometimes check in on the intensity of the schedule: "They'd ask, 'Is this too much? Should we slow down?' But John would overhear and say, 'No, we're good. We're happy to be here.'" Scott would just smile and say, "This is John—we're not slowing down."

Their hectic itineraries took them through cities like London, Paris, Madrid, and Barcelona in just a few days, packed with back-to-back meetings. Despite the demanding schedule, John remained full of energy. "Trust me, he'll run circles around all of us," Scott would reassure their hosts. John was always grateful for their hospitality and never wanted to slow down.

One particular day in Barcelona perfectly captures John's relentless drive. After a full day of meetings, their hosts invited them to celebrate their accomplishments on their last night in Europe. Even though they were out until 1:00 a.m., Scott recalls how John's enthusiasm never wavered, regardless of how intense the schedule had been.

As they got into the car to head back to their hotel, John casually remarked, "Oh, that's right, I've got that TV interview in the morning." Scott, exhausted from the long day, felt a wave of relief when John added, "You don't have to get up at the crack of dawn for that. Don't worry about it."

Grateful for the extra rest, Scott slept in. But when he woke up and turned on the TV, there was John—bright-eyed and energetic—delivering his message with his usual vigor. "That's just who John is," Scott reflects. "If there's someone to talk to, he's there. He's all in, whether it's helping the team or supporting clients. That's always been his way."

John's unwavering energy and drive to connect with clients during those meetings played a key role in Calamos Investments' success. His hands-on approach and commitment to making the most of every opportunity set a strong example for how the company operates, even in the most demanding situations. John wasn't just focused on creating new strategies to meet evolving client needs; he was also rethinking how to best structure the organization to deliver on those goals.

Initially, Calamos Investments operated as "one team and one process," emphasizing collaboration and an integrated approach. "I wanted to maintain that team dynamic where we're all working toward the same goal of supporting our clients," John explained. "But as we grew, I realized we needed to become more specialized to keep up with our expansion."

To reflect this vision, John implemented a "team of teams" structure—one that encouraged collaboration while allowing for specialized expertise. "By focusing on both specialization and teamwork, we can offer the best solutions for our investors," John explained.

This strategic shift enabled the firm to keep innovating and adapting without losing the agility that had driven its early success. With specialized teams focused on specific strategies, they could dive deeper into their areas of expertise. The new structure also gave John the flexibility to explore acquisitions that would enhance the firm's capabilities in line with its core "philosophical approach or DNA," as Scott Becker noted.

The screening process for new teams was intense and exacting. "The 'client-first' mentality has always served us well, and we wanted to ensure that any team we brought on was a strong cultural fit," John explained.

In 2015, Calamos expanded its innovative and alternative strategies with the acquisition of Phineus Partners LP, a hedge fund manager based in San Francisco capitalizing on equity market dynamics, options, and hedging techniques to manage volatility and provide upside participation while limiting downside exposure.

Phineus founder Michael Grant noted, "We were drawn to Calamos for its strong track record in liquid alternatives and our shared investment philosophies, combining rigorous research with secular themes to aim for positive risk-adjusted performance."

Expansion gained significant momentum after John Koudounis joined as CEO in 2016, bringing additional resources to the investment team and creating new growth opportunities for the firm, leveraging his extensive Wall Street experience and relationships.

In 2019, the firm expanded into small-cap investments through its acquisition of Timpani Capital Management, a company that mirrored the client-first mindset John Calamos had established years prior. "At Timpani, we've always prioritized putting our clients first," said Brandon Nelson, Timpani co-founder. "By joining forces with Calamos, my team and I can stay focused on our investment mandates while benefiting from the resources and synergies of a larger, well-established company. We share similar philosophies, embracing active, high-conviction growth investing, and we align on corporate culture and values."

In 2021, the firm acquired Pearl Impact Capital, a team known for its proven investment process. "Risk management has always been at the core of our approach, and we recognized in Pearl Impact Capital a shared commitment to comprehensive risk management," John explained. "They go beyond the numbers, considering nonfinancial risks that many investors tend to overlook."

Risk management continued to drive the firm's latest innovations, including the launch of a private credit solution and a suite of exchange-traded funds (ETFs) designed to offer market participation while providing unique ways to mitigate risk. "Building wealth paves the way to the American Dream," John shared. "That's why we've developed these ETFs; they not only offer investment opportunities but also help investors manage risk effectively as they navigate the markets."

Alongside its financial growth, Calamos Investments has also advanced another cause close to John's heart: philanthropy. In 2023, John Koudounis initiated a strategic partnership with NBA superstar Giannis Antetokounmpo of the Milwaukee Bucks, centered on Pearl Impact's investment expertise. As one of the greatest power forwards in NBA history, Giannis's Greek Nigerian heritage resonated strongly with both Koudounis and John Calamos, especially as they explored joint philanthropic initiatives.

Koudounis met Antetokounmpo through a mutual friend, Marc Lasry, who was an owner of the Milwaukee Bucks and co-founder and CEO of Avenue Capital. While Koudounis was working on a project with Lasry, Marc asked for his help mentoring the young athlete in finance, knowing he could trust Koudounis and that he could speak Giannis's language.

Their first meeting took place in Milwaukee, where Koudounis met directly with Antetokounmpo. Giannis impressed Koudounis not just with his athletic prowess but also with his strong commitment to philanthropy. "What really struck me was his vision for making a difference off the court," John Koudounis explained. Their conversation extended beyond business ventures, focusing on how they could collaborate on community and charitable projects.

This encounter underscored the importance of aligning with individuals who share a commitment to giving back, reinforcing John Calamos's philosophy of blending business success with philanthropy.

Throughout his career, John has adhered to a simple yet powerful idea: constant motion is essential to keep pace with an ever-evolving market landscape. "It's not just about getting bigger;

it's about adapting to the environment we find ourselves in," he remarked, emphasizing the importance of continual adaptation over growth for its own sake.

John's leadership contrasts with that of many contemporaries who set specific growth targets. "Some executives set benchmarks, aiming to reach a certain level by a specific time, but our growth was more organic, dictated by market needs," he reflected, highlighting a philosophy of growth driven by necessity rather than arbitrary goals.

Looking back, John reflected on his journey, admitting he never anticipated the scale of his accomplishments since starting in the 1970s. "I didn't have a set plan like, 'By this date or that, we'll be here.' But it's worked out very well," he mused, recognizing how his success has far exceeded his expectations and enabled him to make a meaningful impact on clients and the industry.

John's story exemplifies how visionary thinking can drive innovation and prosperity. As he looks to the future, he remains committed to fostering an environment where both his firm and clients can thrive, embodying the spirit of progress that has defined his career.

Chapter 23

Forging a Lasting Legacy

John has crafted a formidable legacy in the financial sector through pioneering strategies and visionary leadership at Calamos Investments, and his philanthropic efforts exemplify his belief that successful business leaders must contribute to society.

Echoing Pericles's wisdom that "what you leave behind is not what is engraved on stone monuments, but what is woven into the lives of others," John has left a lasting mark across many walks of life, enriching lives and setting a high standard for future leaders in finance and beyond.

"Describing Dad in one or two words is hard," Laura Calamos, chief administrative officer of Calamos Family Partners, says, reflecting on her father's life. "But if I had to, I'd say he's a 'big picture thinker.' He's also incredibly detail-oriented, ensuring that everything comes together just right."

Her admiration is clear as she describes John's business approach, which goes beyond financial transactions to focus on nurturing relationships and fostering growth not only for the company but also for its employees and clients. "He's always been about more than just making deals; he's about making connections," she notes, illustrating his commitment to building meaningful interactions.

"When I worked as a clerk in the office as a teenager, he told me, 'asset management meant helping families make their dreams come true.' And the company is still doing that every day," she says.

"I've been to meetings across Europe where John's insights and methods are really well respected," says Eli Pars, co-chief investment officer at Calamos Investments, emphasizing John's renowned global reputation in finance. "One of our sales reps attended a meeting in Santiago, Chile, and was surprised to see John's book on convertibles prominently displayed on the attendee's desk."

Eli's remarks highlight the significant impact of John's influence in the financial industry. "It's quite remarkable; many professionals in major banks' convertible training programs are required to read John's book, making it a staple in their curriculum."

This widespread recognition of John's work not only underscores his expertise but also aligns with his guiding philosophy, which Carla D'Antonio emphasizes with a quote he often uses: "Change is like riding a bicycle uphill. If you stop, you're going backwards." She believes this mantra against complacency drives the progressive spirit at Calamos Investments.

"When I started working with John, I was cautious about my job security due to the turnover in the position," Carla recalls. "Now, 20 years later, I owe my longevity to John's leadership style. He makes it easy to work hard for him. He appreciates his team, values our opinions, and ensures we know our ideas matter."

This sentiment is echoed by others on the team. Shannon Hay, senior vice president, Investment Communications, adds, "John isn't just our boss; he genuinely cares about us as individuals. He always checks in and asks about our lives and families, which fosters a strong sense of community and encourages personal growth."

This supportive environment reflects John's thoughtful leadership style. Having closely observed him in action, Carla notes that although his business decisions might seem sudden to outsiders, they are rooted in meticulous research and planning.

"It's difficult to describe the real John," she muses. "He dedicates considerable time to ensure his choices align with the company's long-term goals and positively impacts everyone involved."

Carla hopes that John will long be recognized for both his professional achievements and his personal qualities. "I would love for people to appreciate John as a gifted, incredibly hardworking, supportive, and genuinely kind intellectual," she expresses. "I am humbled and honored to have had the opportunity to work alongside him for so many years."

This sentiment highlights the deep respect John has earned within his company and the profound positive impact he has on those who work closely with him.

John's grandson, Alex Calamos, a wealth advisor at Calamos Wealth Management, fondly reflects on how his grandfather's journey intertwines personal values with professional conduct, profoundly influencing his own life and career. Alex recalls John's inclusive and attentive approach to business, which helped foster a familial culture at Calamos Investments. "He would invite the entire office to significant family events, like my dad's wedding, reinforcing the company's tight-knit community," Alex shared.

This family-like philosophy significantly shaped the company's dynamics. "Watching Grandpa, I learned the importance of really listening—not just waiting to respond but truly understanding what's being said."

Alex explains, "This has become crucial in how I manage my clients' investments." He notes that John's blend of attentive listening and decisive action has instilled in him valuable communication skills essential to his role.

Alex's understanding of his grandfather's impact has deepened his respect and admiration for John's accomplishments. "As I've gotten older, I've started to see the bigger picture of what my grandfather built. People recognize his name, and they respect the funds he pioneered. It's pretty incredible," Alex said.

Echoing this respect, John Koudounis often speaks about John's understated yet profoundly effective leadership style. "Despite his considerable achievements, John has never sought the spotlight," Koudounis explains, his admiration evident. "He has a way of leading that is both quiet and powerful, choosing to let his accomplishments speak for themselves."

In meetings and private chats, Koudounis shares how John's approach not only makes a lasting impression but also demonstrates how his quiet guidance can be a game changer. "There's this subtle strength to him. He watches, he listens, and when needed, he drops insights that can really shift the direction of a project or spark a new strategy," he describes.

These observations not only highlight John's influence but also paint a vivid picture of him as more than just a boss; he is a mentor who values patience and timely wisdom. This leadership style resonates deeply within his family, particularly with Ken Witkowski, John's stepson and senior vice president, director of real estate and business continuity.

Ken admires John's commitment to using his success for meaningful impact, noting, "John has always been dedicated to making his efforts count." He believes that The John P. Calamos Foundation will secure John's enduring legacy.

"Coming from such humble beginnings, John has changed the world and tried to make it a better place for others," Ken remarked. The foundation plays a crucial role in ensuring that John's life's work continues to resonate and impact future generations. To further this mission, John established "Calamos Cares," a team dedicated to organizing charitable activities for associates. These initiatives include supporting military personnel, forest preserve cleanups, meal packaging at food banks, and children's hospitals.

Additionally, Calamos interns participate in their own charitable events during the summer program, fostering a culture of community service that permeates the entire organization. This commitment to giving back reflects John's influence, which has become increasingly evident over the years, both within his firm and the broader financial industry.

Michael Grant, now co-chief investment officer and head of long-short strategies at Calamos, recalls his first meeting with John in 2015. At the time, Michael was leading Phineus Partners LP, where he had successfully launched a long-short investment strategy. He already knew about John's reputation as an innovative investor, and the two were discussing the potential acquisition of Phineus by Calamos. This pivotal moment marked the beginning of his journey with the firm. "John is more than just a financial success; he embodies what Aristotle described as the flourishing life."

This understanding of John's character reveals how his ability to chart his own path, driven by courage and vision, has shaped both his business and the lives of those around him. "He's a dreamer of the day," Michael noted, referencing a favorite passage from T. E. Lawrence's memoir. "John believes in the idea that 'nothing is written,' and that has guided him through the unpredictable world of finance."

Michael also highlighted John's humility and commitment to service, emphasizing that he lives a life focused on others—clients, employees, and the community. "His success isn't just about financial achievements; it's about creating opportunities for others."

Ultimately, John's legacy goes beyond finance. "He exemplifies Aristotle's idea of the good life—active, contemplative, and always serving the wider community," Michael said, reflecting on John's lasting impact on both the industry and the people he's touched.

For nearly two decades, Nick Niziolek, co-chief investment officer and head of global strategies, has witnessed John's unwavering commitment to his guiding principle: always put the client first. "That lesson resonates with me daily," Nick shared. "It sounds simple, but this framework has helped me navigate very complex decisions, and I've seen firsthand how John lives by the principles he preaches." This client-centric philosophy remains a cornerstone of Calamos Investments' culture and strategy, steering the firm through shifting markets and evolving client needs.

Matt Freund, co-chief investment officer at Calamos, spoke about John's impact and what sets him apart, "John always has the investor's best interest at heart. Negative narratives, which often dominate the headlines, may sound compelling, but they frequently underestimate the creativity, productivity, and resilience of the market.

"Throughout his entire career, John has been a positive champion of long-term investing and the ingenuity and wisdom of free markets. Most importantly, he understands and teaches the importance of continuous risk management and the power of looking past short-term volatility. These are the principles investors should focus on to make sound investment decisions."

Tony Tursich, a co-portfolio manager at Calamos, joined the firm in 2021 following its acquisition of Pearl Impact Capital, which he founded. "John has shaped the industry in ways that extend beyond his success in business and investments," remarked Tony. "His positive contribution to society through integrity, pioneering spirit, and generosity will be long-lasting."

Tony has felt the impact of John's leadership firsthand, noting how it resonates throughout the firm and the industry. He believes John's approach to leadership inspires those around him not just to excel in business but to make a meaningful difference beyond it.

Brandon Nelson joined Calamos in 2019 as a senior vice president and senior portfolio manager following the firm's acquisition of Timpani Capital Management, which he cofounded in 2008. Like Michael and Tony, Brandon was attracted to Calamos for its stellar reputation and John's vision, eager to merge his entrepreneurial journey with what John had built. Brandon notes, "Even though he had been doing this for a long time, I was continuously impressed with John's passion and energy for investments, along with his willingness to invest in the firm's future. This is truly his baby."

John's unwavering enthusiasm and dedication to building a client-focused firm that adapts to market challenges form the foundation of his legacy. This legacy encompasses the values he instilled in his team, his relentless pursuit of innovation, and his belief in giving back.

As Tony reflects, "John leads by example, showing us how integrity and innovation endure in business." This commitment to democratizing finance drives Calamos Investments, emphasizing that innovative investment strategies should be accessible to all, not just the most sophisticated investors.

Calamos Investments seizes new opportunities by staying true to its pioneering spirit. In recent years., this has included the firm's expansion into the interval fund space, again providing access for retail investors to participate in strategies once reserved for institutional players.

"Our mantra is to let people who may not have had the chance to invest in these types of products to do so alongside some of the great private equity investors," says John Koudounis. This focus continues as the firm navigates the ever-evolving financial landscape.

Looking ahead, the firm's expansion into the exchange-traded fund space showcases its adaptability. "We are active managers," Koudounis emphasizes, reflecting the firm's commitment to providing options that offer both principal protection and potential upside—an approach rooted in John Calamos's philosophy of innovation coupled with prudent risk management.

As Calamos expands its global presence, enhancing client experiences through technology remains a key focus. "Technology has

Forging a Lasting Legacy

been part of our strategy for years, and we're always refining it," Koudounis notes, highlighting the importance of data analytics and artificial intelligence in personalizing service while maintaining the firm's human touch.

John remains a pivotal figure as the firm evolves in this direction. "He enjoys coming into work every day," Koudounis says. "How can you not when you drive onto this beautiful campus and see everything you've built?"

"John Calamos has established himself as a pioneer in the finance industry. As a leadership team, we take our responsibility to ensure that his name resonates for decades to come very seriously," says Dan Dufresne, Calamos chief operating officer.

Leaders across the industry express deep respect for John's significant impact on asset management. "Many leaders I interact with consistently articulate a reverence for him," Dufresne notes. "I've been fortunate to share quiet moments with him, hearing his stories of valor in service and innovation in finance," Dufresne reflects. "He is truly an impressive and courageous man."

Dufresne believes John embodies the concept of persistent innovation, essential for long-term success. At this stage in his career, with a wealth of accomplishments, he could shift into reflection mode. However, as Dufresne points out, "Far from that, John continues to engage with our team's fresh ideas and is excited about the innovations on the horizon for Calamos."

John's passion for the firm and its values keeps it grounded in his vision of integrity, innovation, and a client-first mindset.

As the financial powerhouse that bears his name approaches its 50th anniversary, he reflects on the past, shaking his head in disbelief. "I can't believe we're nearing 50 years in the business," he shares, pride evident in his voice. This milestone is a testament to decades filled with challenges, triumphs, and invaluable lessons learned.

A key takeaway for John has been the necessity of adapting to change. "You really have to surround yourself with the right people," he explains, emphasizing that success hinges not just on innovative products but also on the dynamic team behind them. "I don't dwell on the past," he says with a chuckle. "Life moves too fast for that!"

John stands proud of what he and his team have built. "This journey isn't just about me; it's about everyone we've helped along the way," he expresses with gratitude. Through Calamos Investments, he has realized his own version of the American Dream while paving the way for countless others to do so as well.

When asked if he has considered retiring anytime soon, John quips, "As I told the *Wall Street Journal* after bringing John Koudounis on board, if I retired, I'd have no excuse for my poor golf game!" This lightheartedness reflects his enduring commitment to the firm and its mission.

With each passing year, John inspires those around him to pursue their financial aspirations, ensuring that the legacy of innovation and integrity will thrive for generations to come. His passion keeps Calamos grounded in the vision he established, with principles of integrity, innovation, and a client-first mindset guiding its future.

Through the leadership of John Koudounis and his commitment to carrying on the vision and high standards of its founder, Calamos Investments is poised to continue thriving as a leader in innovation and responsible investing. "We're running it on John's principles," Koudounis says, ensuring the firm continues to be a beacon of excellence while honoring the man and the vision that has shaped its success.

From the Desk of John P. Calamos, Sr.

One of the most important lessons I've learned is that the road might take you where you least expect it. Even if you don't know where you'll end up, it's crucial to start and keep moving forward. It's okay to change course as you learn more about yourself—what you truly care about and what ignites your passion.

This is especially true when it comes to education. There's a lot of pressure on young people today to pick a specialized major, but I look back at my own journey and see the value in taking a more winding path.

I started at one campus of the University of Illinois, transferred to another, and eventually ended up at Illinois Tech. That was where I was meant to be, and it's been tremendously rewarding to support the incredible work happening there.

I also changed majors more than once. I began as an engineering student, switched to architecture, and ultimately graduated with a degree in economics.

I've never felt that my time in engineering or architecture was wasted; it was simply part of my journey. In fact, I had the chance to return to those roots when it came time to design my first home and, later, the Calamos headquarters in Naperville, Illinois.

Similarly, don't get discouraged if the first career you try doesn't work out. You'll learn a lot about yourself along the way. I've held many different jobs throughout my life, and each one gave me valuable insights into who I was and what mattered most to me. No matter where you are in your career, though, I encourage you to "think like an entrepreneur."

By that, I mean that whether you're a business owner, just starting out, or already in the C-suite, always look for ways to innovate and improve how you serve clients and customers, as well as how you contribute to your team.

Be committed to learning from those around you, and stay intensely curious about the world. This focus on continual improvement, innovation, and learning has been key to my own success, and I've always noticed and appreciated employees who give their all.

My own commitment to learning and improvement, including my view of the markets and the path to investment success, has been shaped by a lifetime of diverse influences and a rich mix of experiences: watching my parents diligently save their modest nest egg, studying philosophy and history in college, serving in the Air Force, staying informed about current events, and spending 50 years growing a business while helping clients achieve their own versions of the American Dream.

So, what advice do I have for future investors navigating the markets in the coming decades?

First and foremost, don't attempt to time the markets. In college, I learned that markets are the pulse of global events, making them both fascinating and unpredictable. Although company performance and earnings are crucial, many other factors come into play.

You must also consider government actions and policies, as these will significantly influence the overall economy and, subsequently, the markets.

Markets are a reflection of economic conditions, political climates, government policies, and geopolitical dynamics, both in the United States and around the world.

For example, the Federal Reserve's actions regarding interest rates and the government's public policy decisions carry significant implications for economic growth, inflation, and market performance.

From the Desk of John P. Calamos, Sr.

Policies that affect small businesses—one of the key drivers of job growth in the United States—have far-reaching consequences for individuals, households, and the overall economy.

In our interconnected global economy, the actions of any individual country can influence others, amplifying the importance of understanding these dynamics.

Being a student of the markets entails more than just studying finance. Because markets reflect the entirety of global occurrences, comprehending them requires a broader perspective that transcends any single academic discipline.

Insights from philosophy and history offer essential context for navigating the complex crosscurrents we face today. This is why I regard my college courses in history and philosophy as some of the most valuable "business" classes I've ever taken.

In addition to history and philosophy, I encourage anyone aspiring to be a better investor to study supply-side economics. This field has provided me with valuable insights into the policies that can foster growth around the globe. Supply-side economics emphasizes the crucial role of innovation in boosting productivity and prosperity across an entire country.

Never underestimate the impact of government policy. The right balance of regulation and taxation can encourage innovation, creativity, and a healthy appetite for risk-taking.

I encourage anyone who wants to learn more about the impact of government on the markets and all of society to read economist Milton Friedman's work, including *Free to Choose*, which he wrote with his wife, Rose. It does an excellent job setting forth the importance of free markets.

Conversely, excessive regulation or tax policies that disincentivize risk can stifle innovation and economic prosperity—for individuals, businesses, and the economy as a whole.

From the Desk of John P. Calamos, Sr.

Globally, we see numerous examples of governments that nurture entrepreneurial spirit and support individual freedoms, as well as those that do not. Over the years, we have witnessed how changes in government policies can swiftly affect economies and, consequently, the markets.

Tax policies play a crucial role in shaping the potential for economic expansion. When tax levels are reasonable, companies can grow and create jobs, providing more people with opportunities to prosper and improve their quality of life.

Both large and small businesses should focus on innovation and be incentivized to discover new and better ways to operate. This pursuit of improvement isn't simply corporate greed; companies need the capacity to reinvest in their operations.

For small businesses, this might mean hiring additional employees, and larger companies might allocate more funds toward research and development—ultimately leading to the next breakthrough technology or medical treatment.

It's the private sector that drives this innovation, not the government. However, it is essential for the government to act as a referee, ensuring that these dynamics flourish without attempting to take control of various industries. These were the ideas that Ronald Reagan espoused so eloquently, and I often reflect on his wisdom.

My success as an investor stems from a forward-looking approach, investing in the future without trying to predict every detail of what will happen.

My perspective on risk has been shaped by my military experience as an Air Force pilot. I learned that although you can't eliminate risk or know precisely how a mission will unfold, you can effectively manage potential risks through preparedness, discipline, and maintaining a cool head.

From the Desk of John P. Calamos, Sr.

Throughout my investment career, I have navigated numerous periods of economic challenges, disruption, and rapid change—experiencing bull and bear markets, raging inflation, and market corrections in the 1970s, Black Monday in 1987, the rise of the internet in the 1990s, the subsequent dot-com bubble of 2000, steep corrections in 2002, the great financial crisis of 2008, and more recently, the global pandemic and the emergence of artificial intelligence. Each of these market conditions presented unique challenges that were impossible to predict in advance.

Successful investors remain open to new approaches. I believe my ability to navigate various market conditions stems largely from my willingness to embrace different strategies and question the status quo—drawing inspiration from Socrates.

When I began my career as an investment advisor in 1970, the financial markets were particularly challenging, with both stocks and bonds under significant pressure. High inflation and interest rates, coupled with an unsettled geopolitical landscape marked by Cold War tensions and conflicts in the Middle East, created an environment ripe for volatility.

Recognizing the need for innovative strategies to manage this volatility became crucial. My studies in risk management and convertible bonds during my time in the Air Force laid a strong foundation for this. This emphasis on managing risks in unique ways has guided my investment philosophy and shaped the strategies we implement at Calamos Investments.

By focusing on forward-looking risk management, we have built a robust framework that includes a diverse range of investment categories, particularly alternatives, to navigate the complexities of the market.

I wish you all the best in life and on your investment journey. May your experiences be both rewarding and successful.

From the Desk of John P. Calamos, Sr.

Acknowledgments

I would like to express my deepest gratitude to John Koudounis, president and chief executive officer. His vision and commitment to celebrating and memorializing the life and career of John Calamos made this book possible.

I want to extend my heartfelt thanks to Carla D'Antonio, vice president of the Office of the Chairman, for her unwavering commitment to this entire endeavor. Without her, this book simply wouldn't have come together.

I also want to sincerely thank Shannon Hay, senior vice president of investment communications. Together with Carla, Shannon offered invaluable editorial insights that truly helped shape this story.

I owe particular thanks to my editor, Colin Madine, for his thoughtful revisions and dedication to making this book as strong and impactful as possible.

I am incredibly grateful to the many Calamos associates for generously sharing their time, experiences, and perspectives, which helped bring this story to life.

Finally, and most important, I extend my gratitude to John P. Calamos, Sr,. whose remarkable journey is at the heart of this book. I truly enjoyed getting to know him, his family, friends, and loyal colleagues, and I am grateful to have been given the opportunity to help share his story.

Thank you all for your support, contributions, and dedication to making this project a success.

—Joe Garner

About Joe Garner

Joe Garner, deemed the "Ken Burns of the written and recorded word" by talk show legend Larry King, is a six-time *New York Times* bestselling author renowned for his innovative storytelling and multimedia approach. His groundbreaking *New York Times* bestselling debut, *We Interrupt This Broadcast*, pairs pivotal historical moments with authentic news broadcasts and features forewords by Walter Cronkite and Brian Williams. Garner has collaborated with celebrated figures across industries, including Academy Award winner Dustin Hoffman, sports broadcast icon Bob Costas, comedy greats Carl and Rob Reiner, and NASCAR Hall of Famer Jeff Gordon. With a unique ability to bring history, culture, and personal legacies to life, Garner remains a leader in the world of nonfiction.

Calamos, John, (*Continued*)
  Motorola factory work, 17–18
  MU-2F flying, 96–97
  National Hellenic Museum
    photo, 185
  newspaper deliveries, 11–12
  New York Stock Exchange
    (photos), 183
  options usage, speech
    (impact), 57
  philanthropy, 131
  philosophy, 153–154
    chair, gift, 132–133
    study, 23–24
  phosphorous rockets, usage
    (Vietnam), 32, 38–39
  photos, 182–184, 187
  ROTC enrollment/training, 19,
    26, 30
  Savage, Terry, interaction,
    59–60
  sorties, flying, 41
  spiritual reliance, deepening,
    35
  stockbroker role, 56–57
  stock certificates discovery,
    13
  technology, importance, 103
  University of Illinois
    acceptance, 18–19
  USAF Captain (photo), 181
  USAF Reserves (photo), 188

  Vietnam
    flight missions, 34
    involvement, 31–39
  Washington Oxi Day
    Foundation photo, 184
  Yuba City home, purchase, 31
Calamos, Jr., John
  birth, 26–27
  photo, 178
Calamos, Laura, 30, 155
  photo, 178
Calamos, Lorraine (Lori), 7
Calamos, Mae, 132
  business partner role, 92
  marriage, 85–87
  photos, 187
  shared values, 93
  working relationship, 92
Calamos, Mary
  influence, 9
  photo, 175
Calamos, Nick, 78, 118
Calamos, Peter, 73–76
  Chicago arrival/survival, 5
  Ellis Island arrival, 3
  Greece return, 74–75
  grocery store, starting/closure,
    6
  Marriage, 7
  photo, 175
  US arrival, 2
Calamos Property Holdings, 91

183

Index

John grew up in Chicago's Austin neighborhood, where the family lived in an apartment above his parents' grocery store, Pete's Food Market. © The John P. Calamos Foundation.

Peter and Mary Calamos worked side by side in their store. © The John P. Calamos Foundation.

The Calamos Family (L to R): sister Lori, father Peter, mother Mary, brother Angelo, and John. © The John P. Calamos Foundation.

John (front row far right), standing at attention as a proud member of the John Hay School Safety Patrol in 1953. © The John P. Calamos Foundation.

Within his first 12 months of intense pilot training at Webb Air Force Base in Texas in 1965, John learned to fly the Northrop T-38 Talon supersonic jet trainer. © The John P. Calamos Foundation.

John transitioned to Beale Air Force Base in California where he trained to fly the B-52 Stratofortress before his deployment to Vietnam. He would again pilot the B-52 for the Strategic Air Command at Minot Air Force Base in North Dakota where the USAF played a critical role in the deterrence strategy during the Cold War. The appearance of U.S. Department of Defense (DoD) visual information does not imply or constitute DoD endorsement.

John, at home in 1968 with his children, Laura and John Jr., while stationed at Beale Air Force Base in California during active duty, just months before being deployed to Vietnam. © The John P. Calamos Foundation, courtesy of Dr. Laura Calamos.

THE UNITED STATES OF AMERICA

TO ALL WHO SHALL SEE THESE PRESENTS, GREETING:

THIS IS TO CERTIFY THAT
THE PRESIDENT OF THE UNITED STATES OF AMERICA
AUTHORIZED BY ACT OF CONGRESS JULY 2, 1926
HAS AWARDED

THE DISTINGUISHED FLYING CROSS

TO

CAPTAIN JOHN P. CALAMOS

FOR
EXTRAORDINARY ACHIEVEMENT
WHILE PARTICIPATING IN AERIAL FLIGHT
28 September 1968

GIVEN UNDER MY HAND IN THE CITY OF WASHINGTON
THIS 31st   DAY OF January   19 69

GEORGE S. BROWN, General, USAF
Commander, Seventh Air Force

Harold Brown
SECRETARY OF THE AIR FORCE

The Distinguished Flying Cross and corresponding citation from President Nixon were among the many honors John received during his military career. © The John P. Calamos Foundation.

CITATION TO ACCOMPANY THE AWARD OF

THE DISTINGUISHED FLYING CROSS

TO

JOHN P. CALAMOS

Captain John P. Calamos distinguished himself by extraordinary achievement while participating in aerial flight as a Forward Air Controller near Thuong Duc Special Forces Camp in Southeast Asia on 28 September 1968. On that date, Captain Calamos flew in support of the Special Forces camp which was under heavy hostile attack. In spite of darkness, marginal weather conditions, and poor visibility, Captain Calamos directed two sets of fighter aircraft, one flare aircraft, and one "Spooky" gunship against the hostile forces. Throughout the four hour mission, hostile forces continuously fired at his aircraft. Due to his outstanding airmanship, the camp was later relieved of the hostile pressure. The professional competence, aerial skill, and devotion to duty displayed by Captain Calamos reflect great credit upon himself and the United States Air Force.

John P. Calamos Sr. in 1969 as a USAF Captain. He retired in 1981 as a Major. © The John P. Calamos Foundation.

Flying for "fun" with fellow reservist, Wendell Green. Wendell and other reservists were some of John's first Calamos Wealth Management clients and remain so to this day. © The John P. Calamos Foundation.

John, shown with his first computer in the mid-1980s, has always been keen to embrace technology. © Calamos Investments LLC, The John P. Calamos Foundation.

As John's reputation grew, he became a popular guest on major networks, sharing his perspectives on market events, risk management, and asset allocation. © Calamos Investments LLC, The John P. Calamos Foundation.

John rings the bell at the New York Stock Exchange to celebrate the 2002 launch of the firm's first closed-end fund. © 2025 NYSE Group, Inc.

Nearly two decades later, John Calamos, John Koudounis, and members of the Calamos team commemorate the launch of the firm's seventh closed-end fund at the Nasdaq. Courtesy of Nasdaq.

John Calamos and John Koudounis maintain a deep connection to their hometown. In 2018, Calamos Investments became the first corporate sponsor to display its logo on the Chicago Bulls court. (Calamos and Koudounis with Michael Reinsdorf, Horace Grant, and Benny the Bull.)

John was the first Vietnam Veteran to be recognized by the Washington Oxi Day Foundation. In his honor, the foundation established the Calamos Service Award to recognize a Vietnam veteran, presented annually at the WWII Memorial. © The Washington Oxi Day Foundation.

Illinois Tech president Raj Echambadi presents John with an honorary doctorate following John's May 2022 commencement speech. (Accompanied by Professor Joseph Orgel and John F. O. Bilson, then John and Mae Calamos Stuart School of Business Dean Endowed Chair.) © Bonnie Robinson Photo.

John, as chairman of the National Hellenic Museum, welcomes over 600 guests at the museum's annual gala in 2024. © Tori Soper.

While studying architecture at Illinois Tech, John came to admire the design philosophy of Ludwig Mies van der Rohe. In 2005, John commissioned Mies van der Rohe's grandson Dirk Lohan to design the Calamos headquarters in Naperville, Illinois. © Calamos Investments LLC, The John P. Calamos Foundation.

John's vision of a corporate campus included construction of a second office building and luxury boutique hotel, Hotel Arista, which would later be complemented by retail, dining, and a high-end apartment complex to complete his "live-work-play" concept. © 2008 James Steinkamp Photography.

John credits his wife Mae as a driving force in their family's success. Her contributions to their real estate, hospitality, and philanthropic endeavors have given him the opportunity to focus on building Calamos Investments. © The John P. Calamos Foundation.

John and Mae celebrate after their vow renewal ceremony in 2015. © The John P. Calamos Foundation, courtesy of Thomas Shockey.

John's friends from the USAF Reserves, pictured here in 2018, join him annually for the Calamos Wealth Management golf outing at Rich Harvest Farms. (L to R: Charlie Pyne, Paul Wagner, Bob Miller, JC Davis, Gene Hall, Wendell Green, Jerry Rich [Owner, Rich Harvest Farms], John Calamos, Len Bochicchio, Dave Harmon.) © Calamos Investments LLC, The John P. Calamos Foundation.